LONDON'S THEATRES

LONDON'S THEATRES

TEXT BY

MIKE KILBURN

PHOTOGRAPHY BY

ALBERTO ARZOZ

FOREWORD BY

ZOË WANAMAKER CBE

NEW HOLLAND

First published in 2002 by New Holland Publishers (UK) Ltd
London • Cape Town • Sydney • Auckland

10 9 8 7 6 5 4 3 2 1

www.newhollandpublishers.com

Garfield House, 86–88 Edgware Road, London W2 2EA,
United Kingdom

80 McKenzie Street, Cape Town 8001, South Africa

14 Aquatic Drive, Frenchs Forest, NSW 2086, Australia

218 Lake Road, Northcote, Auckland, New Zealand

ISBN 1 84330 069 9

Publishing Manager: Jo Hemmings
Senior Editor: Kate Michell
Editor: Gillian Bromley
Editorial Assistant: Anne Konopelski
Designer & Cover Design: Harry Green
Production: Joan Woodroffe
Cartography: William Smuts
Index: Dorothy Frame

Reproduction by
Pica Digital (Pte) Ltd, Singapore
Printed and bound in Singapore by
Kyodo Printing Co. (Singapore) Pte Ltd

COVER AND PRELIMINARY PAGES

FRONT COVER: The sumptuous auditorium and stage curtain of
the Garrick Theatre, as seen from a box, is rich enough to entice
even the most errant theatre-goer to attend a performance at this
fine establishment.

BACK COVER & PAGE 7 (TOP): The Garrick Theatre's loggia, with its
cast-iron tables and chairs, offers a wonderful viewpoint from which
to observe the comings and goings of Theatreland before the start of
an evening performance.

SPINE & PAGE 6 (BOTTOM): Interior decoration in many theatres
often extended as far as the cast-iron row ends, such as this one in
the Victoria Palace Theatre.

HALF-TITLE: The Kirov Opera production at the Royal Opera House,
Covent Garden, of *La Forza del Destino* (The Force of Destiny) by
Verdi. The opera was premiered at the Imperial Theatre, St
Petersburg, on 10 November 1862, and the settings (designed by
Andrei Voitenko) are based on original scenic designs.

FRONTISPIECE: The Willoughby de Broke family crest draws the eye
in this view from a prompt-side box in St Martin's Theatre, whilst
the softness of the swagged house tabs emphasizes the outstanding
quality of the polished walnut interior.

PAGE 5: In the Phoenix Theatre the mirrored ceiling is an inspired
addition to the circular stalls vestibule, which gives access directly
to the auditorium and to a sweeping walkway. The walkway is
enriched by attractive wall mirrors, mid-18th-century decorative
pilasters and acanthus cornicework.

PAGE 6: (TOP) Highly polished reeded brass handrails enhance a
simple staircase in the Albery Theatre; (MIDDLE) One of the
honeysuckle-decorated brass wall ashtrays that adorn St Martin's
Theatre; (BOTTOM) *See above*.

PAGE 7: (TOP) *See above*; (BOTTOM LEFT) The quality of detail inside
the Criterion Theatre is no better highlighted than in the beautiful
draped female figurine that adorns the staircase newel post;
(BOTTOM RIGHT) A quiet corner, embodying the atmosphere
of the 1930s, in the Apollo Theatre.

PAGE 9 Within the ribboned, reeded architrave to the mirrored
recess is a fine console table, and close by a gilded French sofa –
adequately grand for the Royal Retiring Room of the Albery
Theatre.

PAGE 155: The Cambridge Theatre is home to these beautiful
brass-faced doors.

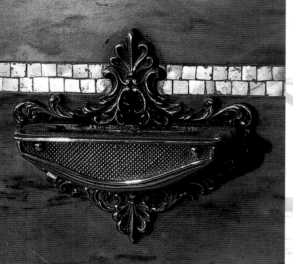

CONTENTS

FOREWORD

What a joy to discover such a magnificent celebration of London's theatres, rich with information and a wealth of dates and facts. This is a book for the true theatre-goer. What a delight to be able to enter all these wonderful establishments by way of these pages; to discover their histories and the very roots of the buildings – a veritable Ordnance Survey map of theatrical London. From the petite perfection of the Donmar Warehouse to the glorious grandeur of Drury Lane – open the pages of this book and your imagination takes flight. Experience the jangle of first-night nerves, the smell of the greasepaint, the plaudits from the stalls, the boos from the gallery, the tears of failure, the joys of success. London possesses the finest concentration of theatres in the world, and here they are for you to enjoy.

Coming from a theatrical family I was taken to the theatre from a very early age, and have crossed the threshold of most theatres in this book. When I first started going to the theatre you could could still rent a stool for the gallery queue – price: '6d'. You went early in the day, paid your money to the attendant, and placed your stool on the pavement as close to the gallery entrance as possible; that reserved you a place in the queue come entry time. Every evening you would see these little crocodiles of seated galleryites all over the West End, a wonderful nightly sight and one that I really miss. It was possible to judge how well the play was doing by the length of this queue. If you got there early enough in the day you could be in the front row of the gallery at night; up in the Gods looking down at the magic below. Now, of course, I am no longer in the gallery looking down, but more often on the stage looking up.

I inherited my passion for the theatre from my father, whose love of the stage was so great that, as a penniless actor in New York, he devised a way of getting to see plays without paying. He would hang about outside the theatre until the interval and then go in with the crowd for the second half. There was a time when he knew the second half of every play on Broadway, but not the beginning! It makes me very proud to know that my father's dream is included in this book – Shakespeare's Globe, which is the oldest as well as the newest theatre in London.

A theatre is essentially a house for entertainment, but it is also a stage for political debate, theological discussion, laughter, tears, anger, romance. All the following playhouses have staged one of the above at sometime – 'tragedy, comedy, history, pastoral, pastoral-comical, historical-pastoral, tragical-historical, tragical-comical-historical-pastoral', as Polonius so delightfully states.

London is home to many beautiful theatres, and this book treasures these, giving a wonderful overall picture. It is a must for any lover of the theatre and an essential attraction for any bookshelf. So many great names, from Garrick to Gielgud, have passed through these stage doors. There are ghosts between these pages, so handle them with care but, above all, enjoy.

Zoë Wanamaker

INTRODUCTION

ondon possesses the finest concentration of theatres anywhere in the world, with visible fabric ranging in date from the early 19th century through to the late 20th. Yet what remains today is a mere fraction of the number of buildings extant 100 years ago, survivals in the face of threats from lucrative office and residential redevelopments, the competing attractions of cinema and television, and road-building proposals in the 1970s. West End theatres entered the 21st century under a cloud, their wellbeing threatened by overpriced tickets and difficult car parking in central London, unfriendly public transport, accusations of physical discomfort in 'outmoded' seating arrangements and, most destructive of all, a dumbed-down world ruled by an unforgiving egalitarianism. But troubled times for the city's stages are nothing new: the evolutionary trajectory of the theatre in London over the centuries has been anything but smooth.

Soon after the Roman invasion of southern Britain by troops of the Emperor Claudius in AD 43, new roads were converging on the site of a wide, navigable river crossing which would quite rapidly develop as Londinium, a multicultural centre of trade and commerce. The capital's history has never been devoid of incident, and it was on this fledgling town that Queen Boudicca and her Iceni tribe descended from their east Anglian heartland – what is now Norfolk – *c.* 1860 to burn and massacre. Notwithstanding such unwelcome setbacks, a port developed commercially and administratively with, by the late 3rd century, a population probably well in excess of 30,000 inhabitants. Archaeology has unearthed extensive topographical evidence revealing landmark buildings such as the Temple of Mithras, the basilica, public and private baths and the governor's palace, but places of entertainment are elusive. Without doubt many of the élite in Roman London, who would have come from Italy, would have been familiar with the great Greco-Roman theatres of Italy, including the Theatre of Marcellus in Rome, or Agrippa's Theatre at Ostia, or even those at Pompeii. However, apart from a 2nd-century multipurpose amphitheatre, demolished in the mid-4th century and now buried under the Guildhall, the City's present administrative centre, nothing of the kind in Roman London has come to light. If there was anything to find, it may well have been obliterated during the past two centuries of basement excavations and the bombing of the First and Second World Wars. By the time the Romans left Britain in the 4th century, theatre was considered to run contrary to the teachings of Christianity, now the official religion of the rulers, so that official theatre buildings were unlikely to have been planned; nevertheless, it may well be that itinerant musicians and players continued to satisfy the citizens' desire for live performance.

The 600-year post-Roman period between *c.* AD 400 and *c.* AD 1000, traditionally and picturesquely referred to as the 'Dark Ages', has been similarly unproductive in terms of archaeological evidence; still, when London moved westwards out of the confines of the Roman town, the itinerant legacy probably persisted. As earthbound diversions were interwoven with ecclesiastical celebrations and mystical rites associated with semi-pagan religious festivals, the ground was laid for the emergence of the 'mystery cycles', sequences of dramas based on

ABOVE The Louis XVI-style plasterwork on the overdoor in Wyndham's Theatre's dress-circle bar draws the eye into one of London's most elegant auditoria.

the location of a particular segment of the play – heaven, hell, earth – evolved by the 16th century into movable wagons: thus the 'pageant' became mobile and could be drawn around the streets of a village or town. Soon, ascents into heaven via a winched cloud or descents into hell via a trapdoor were being achieved, thus laying the foundations of stage machinery.

The later medieval period witnessed the evolution of 'interludes' or short plays performed in the communal halls of great houses, ranging from the royal splendour of Hampton Court to the more lowly Headstone Manor, a moated house owned by the Archbishops of Canterbury which once stood in the open Middlesex fields but is now engulfed in suburbia. These interludes, set within the context of biblical stories, emphasizing heaven and hell, floods and miracles, could be acted out alongside mythological entertainments, often accompanied by musicians. They were performed in front of screens at the service end of the hall, which allowed the players to make maximum use of the cross passageway behind the screens and the multiple doors to the kitchen, buttery and pantry. Their audience, the lord and his guests, would be seated in the normal way at the high table at the opposite end of the hall. So far as the owner of the house was concerned, the drawback of such entertainments was that he was expected to offer a night's 'full board' accommodation to the performers.

In Paris, mystery plays were, by the end of the early 15th century, being performed in a roofed rectangular area of similar proportions to a tennis court. In England, medieval principles of presentation – movable staging on wagons or temporary stages in churches or private houses, rather than any fixed 'stage' – remained the norm until the middle of the 16th century, by which time portable scenery and painted screens were in vogue at court and in a number of great houses. For the actor at this period, the need to be versatile was paramount. Companies of players – usually numbering five, including a boy to take the female parts – plied their trade under the patronage of a lord or even the monarch. They enacted their art in churches, in larger houses or perhaps on trestle tables in the more convivial surroundings of the galleried inn yard – with the strong disapproval of Puritan preachers and London's City Fathers, concerned for public order.

Towards the end of the 16th century London's population was swelled by an influx of persecuted peoples from Europe and English rural dwellers made homeless by economic forces such as the enclosure of common land. In place of villages,

biblical stories or saints' lives, which blossomed in the Middle Ages.

The medieval period is generally considered to extend from the defeat of King Harold at the Battle of Hastings (1066) to the defeat of King Richard III at the Battle of Bosworth (1485). Unsurprisingly, given the dearth of literacy among the populace, there is little secular writing available from these years to shed light on the popular theatre – or, indeed, the lack of it. Ecclesiastical records from the 12th century and even earlier, however, set down staging information and dialogue for the mystery plays, which were often performed in the public parts of a church, rather than impinging upon the clergy's more private domain beyond the rood screen and into the chancel. Settings became more elaborate, until performers were enacting their parts on a raised stage, which lifted them into a position where the audience, or congregation, could clearly see the action. Multiple stages, each representing

fields and smallholdings the suburbs grew up, a phenomenon accompanied by a sharp rise in literacy. A turbulent political arena saw Queen Elizabeth I excommunicated by Pope Pius V in 1570, and Mary, Queen of Scots, manoeuvring to replace her on the English throne. Against this

ABOVE The plaster trophy and ornate mirror are enhanced by the simplicity of paired Ionic pilasters in the Strand Theatre. It is this architectural emancipation that is the springboard of early 20th-century theatre architecture.

backdrop the actor and carpenter James Burbage built in 1576 what may have been the first public theatre. Known as the Theatre in the Liberty of Holywell, it stood close to the modern junction of Great Eastern Street with Curtain Road in the borough of Hackney, with the slightly later (1577) Curtain Theatre a little to its south. The timber buildings were multifaceted, probably octagonal or polygonal, their design inspired by the animal-baiting pits familiar around the capital.

Of the 20 or so theatres built in London during the next 40 years a high proportion were situated outside the City walls, in order to escape the heavy

guiding hand of the City Fathers. The Globe, the Swan, the Fortune and the Rose were grouped close to Southwark Cathedral on the south side of the Thames. It was the excavation of the Rose in 1989 that provided the first comprehensive analysis of the fabric of an Elizabethan theatre, so invaluable in the planning and building of the replica timbered Globe on Bankside – an exercise presenting an unexpected challenge to the ingenuity of the 20th-century master craftsmen involved. When Johannes de Witt came to England from Holland in 1596, he little knew that he would leave behind him a drawing of inestimable importance, showing the interior of the Swan. This single sketch depicted with amazing care, although so valuable, made little constructional sense when applied to the reconstruction of the Globe.

Theatres such as the Swan, the Rose and the Globe provided facilities to accommodate and nurture a stable audience of up to 3,000 for theatre in London. Actors such as Richard Burbage and Edward Alleyn could amass a considerable following, from which sometimes prohibitively expensive entrance fees excluded, for the most part, the less privileged. Free entertainment could always be had at public executions! In competition with bear-baiting and cockfighting, Elizabethan theatre flourished, not only, as it would so often appear, in the plays of Shakespeare at the Globe, where he was active for some ten years, but also through the works of Ben Jonson (1572–1637), Edmund Spenser (1552–99) and Christopher Marlowe (1564–93).

In the mode of present-day television satire or tabloid headlines, early 17th-century theatre was not averse to pointing out royal failings and the disaster that could so easily result from royal unpopularity with the masses. During the English Civil Wars of the 1640s and 1650s London was the stronghold of Parliamentarianism, and in 1642, 1647 and 1648 closure orders were issued on the theatres, probably as a result of a genuine concern to avoid the disorder likely to erupt at public meetings – particularly in the run-up to the trial of Charles I. However, theatre was never totally suppressed and continued, albeit in limited fashion, throughout the Commonwealth; and the restoration of the monarch in 1660, in the person of the rumbustious King Charles II, heralded a resurgence of drama in London. Architecturally, this was a period of great achievement and equally great disaster: Inigo Jones and John Webb were working on the building of The Queen's House at Greenwich and Greenwich Hospital, and in 1666 the old St Paul's Cathedral was lost in the Great Fire of London.

Of tremendous significance in the development of the theatre in London was the granting by the King in 1662 of two royal patents to William D'Avenant and his Duke's Company and to Thomas Killigrew and his King's Company, which, in effect, established a monopoly, treasured and

ABOVE A single lunette and a pair of seated muses sit within the saucer-dome that dominates the auditorium ceiling of the Queen's Theatre.

guarded by their descendants. The patents are discussed below in the chapters on the Royal Opera House and Theatre Royal, Drury Lane. Also of importance is the broader influence of the restored monarchy on the theatre, for Charles II – 30 years old when he mounted the throne – had spent his formative years seeking compensation for his exile from England in the pleasures of life on the European mainland. Thus he absorbed, and brought back to England, French and Italian theatrical developments, including the new changeable perspective scenes and the use of women rather than boys to play female parts – a move that proved

to be very popular. From now on stage machinery played an ever-increasing part in theatrical spectacle, providing cloudscapes, seasonal landscapes and seascapes, and the magical appearance and disappearance of actors as required. As the depth of vista increased with the number of painted flats (supported and sliding in grooves), so the stage moved forward into the audience, introducing a previously unknown intimacy, to such an extent that members of the audience might occupy part of the stage during a performance. The dominant form of theatrical performance at this time was the bawdy comedy of manners, staged for a fashionable rather than a popular audience.

The creation of only two patent houses was a serious hindrance to a pleasure-seeking public with a taste for theatre, and it is hardly surprising that by the beginning of the 18th century John Vanbrugh was designing and building the Queen's Theatre in the Haymarket (now Her Majesty's Theatre). This was followed in 1720 by the Haymarket Theatre (now the Theatre Royal), funded by a local carpenter – although it was to be 40 years before the unlicensed Haymarket Theatre received a limited, summer-only patent. In the meantime it put on unlicensed plays, and to an extent a blind eye was turned to its technically illicit activity.

Through the 18th century and into the 19th, the population expansion of London continued as agricultural workers, particularly in the Midlands, were forced in increasing numbers from their villages by avaricious landlords who replaced their small fields and accessible common land with large, enclosed, sheep-filled pastures. Seeking new skills away from a diminishing agricultural market – sometimes in nearby towns, but especially in London – this homeless workforce fuelled the capital's industrial expansion, becoming an urban class with disposable income from which it could easily be parted in pubs or, better still, at the theatre.

Making up for their paucity of numbers by the ingenuity with which they overcame the legal restrictions on their activity, unlicensed theatres thrived during the opening decades of the 18th century in response to public demand. Built for short-term profit rather than long-term durability, many of the theatre structures built from the late 17th century to the early 19th were unstable and extremely susceptible to fire, often resulting in huge loss of life: two notable examples of such disasters were those that destroyed the Theatre Royal, Drury Lane, and the Lyceum in Wellington Street.

The 1737 Licensing Act confirmed the monopoly of the patent theatres and curtailed the expansion of unlicensed houses, authorizing the Lord Chamberlain to act as censor, with the responsibility to decree which plays could or could not be performed – a role he retained until well into the 20th century. To avoid the stringent regulations applying to all performances for which entry fees

ABOVE In the former Grand Saloon, now the elegant dress-circle bar, of the Gielgud Theatre, the air of spaciousness was achieved by architect W. G. R. Sprague at the peak of his powers.

were charged, 'free' concerts were organized – with the understood proviso that the audience should buy small items at the door or during the interval to cover costs. For the performers, the keyword was still versatility. The programme mix was an ingenious amalgam of pantomime, drama, music and dance, requiring a depth and breadth of ability in both actors and musicians. Eventually the various elements of these mixed performances separated out to become popular entertainments in their own

right: the melodrama, music hall, theatre and burlesque of the 19th century.

It is tempting to hope that in the West End or even Greater London there may be a building to rival the Theatre Royal, Bristol (1766) or the Georgian Theatre of Richmond, Yorkshire (1788), but as yet nothing is visible from such early dates – in fact, nothing is visible from before 1812. No doubt one day archaeology will reveal the pre-19th-century fabric at Theatre Royal, Drury Lane, or Covent Garden, or at the Lyceum or the Theatre Royal, Haymarket, to flesh out the documentary, verbal and visual evidence that is all we have at present.

The 18th century, and to an even greater extent the 19th, witnessed the rise of the specialist within the design and everyday working of the theatre. In the Midlands and London, the shadowy figures of Mr Evans, and, later, Mr Roberts (of Nottingham) and Mr Goodger (of the Surrey Theatre in Lambeth and the Theatre Royal in Leicester) were constructing stage machinery, fulfilling the increasing demand for spectacular transformation and illusionary scenes, now almost forgotten. Mr Herbert of Manchester was painting drop scenes, while Mr Earle of London specialized as a scenic figure painter. These men, referred to respectfully by E. M. Forster as the 'elder race', were craftsmen, carpenters and wheelwrights who took pride in their hard-won knowledge.

It is, however, the parallel rise of the architect and the flamboyant entrepreneur that is particularly striking during the later decades of the 19th century. In 1843 the Theatres Act broke the stranglehold of the patent houses, opening the way to a new generation of construction. Often building on awkward sites, these innovators overshadowed the achievements of men such as Thomas W. Grieves, who were tackling problems and taking out patents on matters such as improved fire safety and improved structural stability of stages. The plays of Oscar Wilde and the operettas of Gilbert and Sullivan in turn drew admiring crowds; on stage, Sir Henry Irving, Charles Wyndham, Mary Moore and Ellen Terry were idolized. Certainly there was no lack of theatres of one sort or another by the end of the 19th century: in her indispensable reference book *London Theatres and Music Halls, 1850–1950*, Diana Howard identifies 910 places of entertainment in the capital, ranging from public houses to purpose-built theatres.

A number of high-calibre architects, such as T. E. Collcutt, the brothers William and Thomas Ridley Milburn, and in more recent times John and Sylvia Reid, worked on only one West End theatre apiece. In contrast, three 'people's architects', Frank

Matcham, C. J. Phipps and W. G. R. Sprague became to the theatre of the late 19th and early 20th centuries what today Sir Norman Foster and Lord Richard Rogers have become to architecture more generally in the City and beyond.

Frank Matcham was, without any doubt, Britain's

ABOVE Polished woodwork trimmed with gold provides an understated air of opulence in the walkway to the dress-circle bar in the Theatre Royal, Haymarket – another masterpiece by W. G. R. Sprague.

most eminent theatre architect. Between the mid-1870s, when he joined the practice of J. T. Robinson (whose daughter Maria he subsequently married), and 1913, when he made alterations to his Moorish-style Palace Theatre, Leicester (demolished in 1960 to make space for offices), he designed, reconstructed or rebuilt over 150 theatre buildings throughout the British Isles. As he retired cinema was coming into vogue, and his firm, Matcham and Co., would ironically go on to design and build for an industry that was to threaten the very existence of live theatre. A man of action all his life, he suffered a curious and tragic death at the early age of 66 in 1920, from blood poisoning caused by the over-zealous cutting of his fingernails!

Eleven years younger than Matcham, W. G. R. Sprague was articled to the senior architect for four years before joining Walter Emden's practice and subsequently going on to design and build over 30 theatres, including eight in the West End and another ten in London's suburbs. A Francophile at heart, Sprague produced designs whose elegance and restraint in the use of classical motifs are lacking in Matcham's bolder approach. He worked

on into the early flowering of Art Deco, dying at the age of 69.

The third member of this theatrical triumvirate, C. J. Phipps, was born near Bath in 1835 and articled to local architects Wilson and Puller before setting up his own practice in 1857. In 1862 he rebuilt the Bath Theatre so successfully that over the ensuing three decades some 70 theatre commissions followed. Another Francophile, he imparted a restrained, almost dignified tone to his work which stood in marked contrast to Matcham at his most vibrant. Phipps died suddenly at the age of 62.

In a world where Victorian morality had taken about itself a girdle of unforgiving harshness, it would be fascinating to enter the mind of the average, apparently staid paterfamilias as he and his family took their seats in one of the decorative West End auditoria. Few recorded their thoughts, but, surrounded by a plethora of naked or semi-naked men and women in the form of gods and goddesses or fauns and satyrs, they must, to say the very least, have experienced a 'culture shock' of the first order.

Today we have a Royal National Theatre on the South Bank, and a handful of late-20th-century houses which it seems to have fathered. But just when the theatre should be celebrating a triumph, it is looking tentatively over its shoulder for threats to the supreme visual art. It is not world war or, indeed, the advent of cinema that has presented the possibility of slow extinction: it is television, with its alluring offer of non-stop armchair entertainment, and its ability to allow more people to see a single episode of a soap opera than have seen *The Mousetrap* in 20 years. Without doubt tourism currently plays a huge part in the ongoing success of the West End theatre; but as virtual reality, the Internet and the computer come to govern increasing hours in the lives of an increasing number of people, this may be only a temporary respite. Sadly, supremely high-quality productions cannot be relied upon to sustain public interest; often, indeed, the reverse is true. Inescapably, at the final reckoning it is the public who will decide the future of the live theatre as the 21st century progresses; and as costs mount for even a modest production, risk-taking is not high on any financier's agenda. Perhaps the last word belongs to Samuel Johnson (1709–84), who wryly acknowledged in his Prologue to the opening of Drury Lane Theatre:

The stage but echoes back the public voice,
The drama's Laws, the drama's patrons give,
For we that live to please, must please to live.

ADELPHI THEATRE
STRAND

ABOVE Immediately recognizable as 1930s Art Deco, this beautiful faceted foyer lighting epitomizes a decade of simple elegance.

RIGHT The very English quality of Schaufelberg's advert-hung façade, with its bold but comparatively simple interpretation of Art Deco, prompts reflection on the Chicago of Louis Sullivan and Frank Lloyd Wright.

ntil the middle of the 16th century the Strand was an unpaved Thames-side path, bordering on one side a wider, unembanked river and on the other the gardens of grand houses. By the early 17th century those buildings had been demolished, to be replaced by smaller houses and fashionable shops; and during the 1830s the Strand's western end was remodelled by architect John Nash. But it was in the latter half of the 19th century and the early decades of the 20th that the greatest transformation took place, as a comprehensive redevelopment programme removed many of the early buildings. Changes on a colossal scale, including the building of Shaftesbury Avenue and Charing Cross Road, altered the face of the West End, in the process providing sharp-witted entrepreneurs with an opportunity to buy or lease vacant plots upon which to build theatres.

The Adelphi was not part of this rush to secure promising money-making sites, as the theatre, in a variety of configurations, had been in place since 1806. Known originally as the Sans Pareil, it was founded by John Scott, who made his fortune with his invention of a washing blue, known as 'Old True Blue', which he sold along with magic lanterns in his shop in the Strand. It was Scott's talented, stage-struck daughter, Jane Margaret, who encouraged her father to establish a 'well-appointed house' at the rear of his shop. Seats were not cheap: Scott asked 5 shillings for box seats and 3 shillings in the pit (though both prices were subsequently reduced by 1 shilling).

The theatre was such a great success that Scott enlarged the auditorium in 1813–14 by the purchase of adjacent plots of land, and built a columned portico on the Strand. In 1819 he sold the building to T. Willis Jones and the playwright J. T. G. Rodwell, and, renamed the Adelphi, it continued to prosper. The frontage was rebuilt in 1840 to the designs of Samuel Beazley, architect of the Royal Lyceum (1816; burnt down 1830) and the interior of the Theatre Royal, Drury Lane (1822).

Over the ensuing years the building was remodelled. In 1834 No. 18 Maiden Lane (built around 1635) had been acquired to accommodate enlargement of the stage by the owners Frederick Yates and Daniel Terry; and additional boxes were added. In 1858 another rebuilding programme produced an archetypal three-tier auditorium with a capacity of some 1,400. In 1878 restaurateurs Agostino and Stefano Gatti bought the theatre lease from Benjamin Webster and F. B. Chatterton, also acquiring in 1885 the adjacent properties Nos. 409 and 410 Strand – where architect Spencer Chadwick built the Adelphi Theatre Restaurant, which opened in 1887 – and in 1891 No. 20 Maiden Lane, dating from c. 1635; a plaque on this house records the murder by a stagehand of the famous actor William Terris on 16 December 1897.

The year 1900 saw the lease pass to George Edwards, manager of the Gaiety in the Strand, who with architect Ernest Runtz virtually rebuilt the theatre for the production of musical comedy, at the same time enlarging the access from the Strand. The most recent rebuilding took place in 1930, when the theatre was entirely reconstructed to designs by Ernest Schaufelberg, retaining of the former structure only the flank walls and houses at Nos. 18–20 Maiden Lane, which had been refaced in 1868.

the theatre from 1937, producing plays and revues until 1950, when Jack Hylton acquired the lease. A fine bust of Cochran by Peter Lambda graces his former office, now the upper-circle bar.

Within the theatre fragmentary remnants of former builds survive, probably of the early to mid-19th century, in the basement workshops and in 'lost corners' where steps and wall decoration survive. During the late 1950s and early 1960s the theatre was threatened with redevelopment, but a wise London County Council threw out the proposals; in 1955 the site of the Adelphi Restaurant was sold to F. W. Woolworth and Co., and an abortive attempt was made to demolish the theatre in order to build a store; the attempt was repeated by City

ABOVE LEFT This striking horizontal octagonal window lights the dress-circle bar. The chrome and fluted glass light reflects the style of the window.

ABOVE RIGHT
Schaufelberg's dignified auditorium shows the angular, unmistakable voice of the 1930s. Two concrete-framed, cantilevered balconies allow uninterrupted sight lines.

Schaufelberg's *moderne*, now painted façade on the Strand is faced in gridded white faience tiles on a black base; the theatre's name runs along the parapet in large capital letters, an addition of 1937. The long, rectangular, typically Art Deco foyer is lined in black marble under a stepped angular ceiling. The straight-sided, angular auditorium, with two concrete-framed cantilevered balconies, is very much of its age, and of considerable importance in the evolution of Art Deco in cinema and theatre design. Polished wood, marble and chromium feature strongly in Schaufelberg's scheme, originally highlighted by the use of gold, orange, green and dusky pink. The theatre was provided with a cinema projection room, and the installation of a stage revolve (removed in 1993) was initiated by C. B. Cochran, who managed

Centre Properties in 1960, but permission was again refused by the council. Today, however, the restaurant is occupied by an amusement arcade.

The mid-19th century saw a series of dramatizations of Charles Dickens's novels staged at the Adelphi, and in 1867 *No Thoroughfare*, by Dickens and Wilkie Collins, had a successful run. In more recent times the magnificent Marie Tempest gave her final London performance here in *Dear Octopus* (1940), and Ivor Novello's *The Dancing Years* ran for almost 1,000 performances in 1942. In 1958 *Auntie Mame* was followed by *Blitz!*, and in 1965 *Charlie Girl* ran for 2,000 performances. *Showboat*, *The King and I*, *Me and My Girl* and *Chicago* have added to the long list of successful productions staged at the Adelphi.

ALBERY THEATRE
ST MARTIN'S LANE

HISTORY

- 1903. Theatre opens, designed by W. G. R. Sprague for Charles Wyndham and Mary Moore, and named the New Theatre.

- 1973. Renamed Albery Theatre.

- Statutorily Listed Historic Building: Grade II.

OF SPECIAL INTEREST

- A theatre tightly planned with great skill on a restricted site.

- An uncommonly good Louis XVI interior.

- Seating capacity: 878.

ABOVE The highly polished reeded brass handrail enhances an otherwise simple staircase.

RIGHT Coupled half columns, portrait medallions of French kings and queens, and ormolu tripod lamps are individual ingredients brilliantly drawn together by W. G. R. Sprague in this out-standing Louis XVI auditorium of 1903.

t Martin's Lane probably originated as a medieval field road extending from St Martin-in-the-Fields and the Strand in the south to St Giles-in-the-Fields (close to the Shaftesbury Theatre) in the north. For 200 years from the early 17th century the rich and famous took up residence in grand houses, mainly on the west side of the Lane, in an enclave that attracted the great and the good of the arts world of Britain and Europe. They included Sir Joshua Reynolds, who became first President of the Royal Academy in 1768, and Louis Roubiliac, a French-born sculptor of extraordinary genius who set up his studio here in 1738. Along the east side, opposite to where the Albery now stands, were the premises of various craftsmen and artisans: Thomas Chippendale's workshop, now marked by a London County Council blue plaque, occupied a site here during the second half of the 18th century, manufacturing restrained rococo, Chinese and Gothic furniture for a demanding market. Avoiding excessive ornament in his designs, Chippendale relied on form and proportion to achieve his elegant effects, and had he been able to revisit St Martin's Lane around 12 March 1903, when the New Theatre opened, he would have been pleased with what he saw.

On the west side of St Martin's Lane, the theatre sits well between The Salisbury public house and the rebuilt Westminster County Court of 1908, designed with considerable skill in a free classical style by H. N. Hawks of the Office of Works, faced with Portland stone and adorned with decorative carving by Gilbert Seale. Justice is no longer dispensed here, only food and drink: it is now Browns Restaurant. In 1899 Charles Wyndham and Mary Moore had

same architect that he turned to design the New – but in a rather more expansive mode, in collaboration with interior design consultant Claude Ponsonby. Consisting of three major bays, and three and four storeys in height, the Portland stone faced building is a fine piece of eclectic free classical design, with the large central, slightly advanced bay, under a bold pediment and ornamented tympanum, flanked by balustraded parapets and ball finials on dies. The façade is articulated by giant Ionic pilasters extending through the first and second storeys, with an arcaded loggia at first-floor level fronting the grand-circle bar. The flank elevation is faced in white and brown glazed brick, with yellow stock brick to the rear. An original, very pretty, cast-iron decorative bracketed canopy extends across the front of the building and, in a simplified form, down its side.

Fine polished timber entrance doors open onto an interior of surprising sensitivity and almost domestic delicacy, contrasting with the correct classical form of the façade. Pale apricot, blue and gold bring to life a marble-floored Adamesque foyer. Corinthian pilasters support a simple cornice, the whole being dominated by a guilloche-circled ceiling. Emphasizing the room's domestic character is a white marble chimneypiece with a sunburst central ornamental panel. Immediately above, the grand-circle bar with its swagged wall decoration and deeply coved ceiling is amazingly generous on a restricted site, where every square foot of space within the auditorium has been allocated by careful planning.

The restrained Louis XVI auditorium is a joy. On a base colour of pale grey, gold highlighting has been used with an unusually light touch. Bombé-fronted balconies curve sinuously in varying forms, ornamented with beautiful painted panels, ormolu lamps and sconces. Three-tier stage boxes are formed within the reveal of the square proscenium arch, which is capped by relief figures representing music and peace. Completing the French flavour of the auditorium are portrait medallions of French kings and queens.

In 1924 a very young Sybil Thorndike packed the theatre with her portrayal of St Joan in George Bernard Shaw's masterpiece. During the 1930s and 1940s John Gielgud and Laurence Olivier were regular performers here, and it is said that Olivier's much-publicized relationship with Vivien Leigh started at the New Theatre. *Under Milk Wood* was on stage in the mid-1950s and *Oliver!* in the 1960s. In the 1980s *Children of a Lesser God* and Willy Russell's *Blood Brothers* made a considerable impact on London's theatre audiences.

ABOVE The eclectic free classical front elevation is dominated by a wide pediment, incorporating a carved tympanum. The delicate ironwork of the canopy, glimpsed bottom left, may be original to the building.

opened Wyndham's Theatre, fronting onto Charing Cross Road, but it was as Sir Charles – he was knighted in 1902 for services to the theatre – that Wyndham opened his New Theatre, built back-to-back with a bridge link to Wyndhams on land he had been forced to lease as part of his original deal with the Marquess of Salisbury. Had he been able to sell the 'left-over' plot, there would have been no New Theatre. The theatre's name changed in 1973 to honour the memory of Sir Bronson Albery, son of James Albery and Mary Moore.

To design his first theatre Charles Wyndham had commissioned W. G. R. Sprague, and it was to the

ABOVE It is the quality of the undramatic but highly polished woodwork, bevelled glass and plasterwork that produces the effect of an unusually audience-friendly foyer.

LEFT Above the proscenium, a beautiful ensemble of Peace and Music is flanked by cupids in the guise of Summer and Winter. Originally the group, with curtains (no longer there) of dusty pink brocade and velvet, produced an air of opulence within the auditorium.

ALDWYCH THEATRE
ALDWYCH

HISTORY

• 1905. Theatre designed by architect W. G. R. Sprague for actor–manager Seymour Hicks.

• Statutorily Listed Historic Building: Grade II.

OF SPECIAL INTEREST

• The exemplary care given by Sprague to developing his elevational treatment of the theatre.

• The sensitive, elegant design of the interior.

• The rare survival of a private lavatory, now purely decorative, to one dress-circle box.

• Seating capacity: 1,096.

ABOVE The free-standing Ionic columns greatly contribute to the elegant quality of the dress-circle bar.

OPPOSITE Banks of lights suspended from the balconies fail to quash the elegant spirit of the auditorium.

ldwych, the sweeping crescent link opened in 1905 between the Strand and Kingsway, springs at its western end from the foot of Waterloo Bridge, while its eastern extreme is marked by the church of St Clement Danes, designed by Christopher Wren in 1679 and altered 40 years later by James Gibbs. To build the new street a vast swathe was cut through the ancient timber-framed and later buildings at the southern end of Drury Lane, Catherine Street and Wych Street, including several theatres: the already closed Globe and Opera Comique (known as 'The Rickety Twins' on account of their somewhat ramshackle build); the Olympic, designed by Bertie Crewe and W. G. R. Sprague in 1890; and the Gaiety, designed by C. J. Phipps in 1868. The most disastrous loss, however, came half a century later, when the New Gaiety closed in 1957. Designed in 1903 by architects Ernest Runtz and George McLean Ford, with elevations by Norman Shaw – an architect rather more famous for his work in Bedford Park, Chiswick, and for his country houses – it stood in a prominent position overlooking the bridge approach. After closure the New Gaiety was demolished and replaced by the somewhat less attractive Citibank House.

The Aldwych Theatre, situated at the foot of Drury Lane, opened on 23 December 1905. The Strand, sited on the angle with Catherine Street, preceded it by seven months. W. G. R. Sprague designed the two theatres as a complementary, almost matching pair, reminiscent of his paired theatres in Shaftesbury Avenue, the Gielgud (formerly the Globe) and the Queen's. Between the two buildings, and dating from 1908, is A. G. R. Mackenzie's rather over-scaled Beaux-Arts classical Waldorf Hotel, seven storeys high and stone-faced; a giant Ionic order is capped by panels of frolicking cherubs between end pavilions. Mackenzie also designed Australia House in Aldwych. In otherwise architecturally bland surroundings, Bush House, almost opposite the theatre, has an interesting history. Designed for Irving T. Bush by American architects Helme and Corbett in 1935, it was intended as a manufacturer's showplace, where the best of US products would be exhibited; but Bush's dream was never realized, and by 1940 the building had become the home of part of the British Broadcasting Corporation. Towards the foot of Drury Lane is St Clement Danes School, founded in 1700 but rebuilt in 1907 in an up-to-date style. The rear of the theatre is dominated by 'feature' iron fire-escape staircases for the Waldorf Hotel.

Designing corner buildings can be extremely difficult, but Sprague was a master of the art, as he demonstrates here with his Portland-stone free classical façade, tinged with the Beaux-Arts traditions that found fuller expression in the Waldorf Hotel. The ground and first floors, in a building consisting of four storeys plus attics, form a rusticated podium supporting matching elevations on Aldwych and Drury Lane. A giant engaged Ionic order rises through the second and third storeys to pediments on each main elevation, and the attic storeys are crowned by swagged ball finials and statuary groups representing music and theatre. The bowed corner link is a subtle continuation of the established theme, tied together by a long ground-floor canopy.

From the street entrance a semi-elliptical vestibule leads into an extremely lively two-storey foyer ornamented by Ionic pilasters, swagging decorated with

the present colour scheme of deep bluey-green and gold takes nothing away from the quality of the conception, the whole being contained under a coffered white and gold dome. Although the Royal Shakespeare Company damaged the stalls boxes during its residence in the theatre from the 1960s to the 1980s, by partially removing the fronts and painting out the decoration, they have since been restored to the original style, and their decorative theme is maintained in the elliptical ante-room to one dress-circle box. A wonderful survival is a private lavatory to this box, complete with its original green, flowered tiles, and an array of angry birds at cornice level.

The theatre opened with actor–manager Seymour Hicks and his wife Ellaline Terriss starring in the musical *Blue Bell*, which was followed by musical comedies and drama. The theatre is most widely remembered for Ben Travers' 'Aldwych farces' of the 1920s and early 1930s, including *A Cuckoo in the Nest*, *Thark* and *Turkey Time*. Between 1960 and 1982 the Royal Shakespeare Company staged, among many other productions, the highly successful *Becket* (1961) and *Nicholas Nickleby* (1964).

ABOVE This part-elevation clearly illustrates W. G. R. Sprague's skill in designing a building that successfully turns the corner into Drury Lane.

ABOVE The dress-circle bar has a splendour and ambience that would not be out of place in a country house.

reliefs of fruit and modillion cornicework. The triple entrance doors embrace the baroque with cartouche and urn decoration, while the main staircase is decorated with ribboned bay leaf on a closed string with egg and dart capping. At first-floor level, overlooking the foyer, is the former smoking room, now the dress-circle bar.

The twin-balconied auditorium, described in the trade press as Georgian – although, like a number of 19th-century theatres, it uses 18th-century themes and ornamentation in a playful fashion rather than aiming at a strictly authentic 18th-century style overall – is an essay in elegance. Originally decorated in cream, gold and crimson,

APOLLO THEATRE
SHAFTESBURY AVENUE

HISTORY

- 1900. Site purchased by Henry Lowenfeld.

- Theatre designed by Lewen Sharp.

- Statutorily Listed Historic Building: Grade II.

OF SPECIAL INTEREST

- Façade on Shaftesbury Avenue in free Renaissance style with Art Nouveau overtones.

- Interior in Louis XIV style.

- Seating capacity: 775.

ABOVE This remarkably lifelike draped male figure forms part of the auditorium decoration by Messrs Hooydonk.

RIGHT The highly decorated auditorium is made livelier still by the inclusion of smiling, audaciously semi-naked figures.

s early as the 1860s proposals to improve traffic movement between Charing Cross and Tottenham Court Road were being seriously considered at government level. It was not until 1877, however, that the Metropolitan Street Improvements Act authorized the Metropolitan Board of Works to create Charing Cross Road and Shaftesbury Avenue. Under the direction of architect George Vulliamy and engineer Sir Joseph Bazalgette, the proposals were to be achieved as far as possible through street widening rather than wholesale demolition. However, Shaftesbury Avenue – the southern end of which was envisaged as sweeping into Piccadilly Circus, bounded by buildings matching in design quality those on the Regent Street Quadrant – would have to run through some of London's worst slums, the eyries of Dickens's novels, and the street works were held up by the need to rehouse thousands of residents. Not until 1884 was the rehousing requirement of the 1877 Act achieved and the demolition works put in hand, accompanied almost inevitably by accusations of dishonesty and enquiries into the disposal of lands. The fact that the Board of Works was careful with its money, hanging onto land until a buyer was found, allowed the Apollo site to remain in private ownership until it was purchased in 1900 by Henry Lowenfeld as a prime theatre location adjacent to the Lyric, which had opened some 12 years earlier.

Lowenfeld commissioned architect Lewen Sharp to produce his new

does not flag, through to the very pretty blue and white glazed decorative tiles that enliven the otherwise dull dressing-room staircase and which appear to be original. The auditorium, originally decorated in white and gold with crimson panels in a Louis XIV style, offers a home to a proliferation of cherubs and cupids. The colour scheme is now a warmer peachy pink, and the wall panels are pale green, under a mainly cameo blue, richly ornamented, shallow-domed ceiling. Sea gods in washed-out colours fill the tympanum above a proscenium arch flanked by richly ornamented tiers of boxes. Minor alterations carried out in 1932 by Ernest Schaufelberg, architect of the Adelphi Theatre, have not diminished the quality of the architecture.

Henry Lowenfeld, as owner–manager, announced a competition for the name of his new theatre, with

ABOVE LEFT Draped female figures flirt with Art Nouveau on Lewen Sharp's free Renaissance elevation to Shaftesbury Avenue.

ABOVE RIGHT This fine, rather haughty bird is typical of the high-quality plasterwork found in the auditorium.

building. On the face of it this was an odd choice, for Sharp had no experience of theatre design, but Lowenfeld's confidence was well rewarded. Sharp's almost symmetrical stone-faced façade on Shaftesbury Avenue is an exuberant essay in free Renaissance style, the eye-catching pairs of winged, draped female figures sculpted by T. Simpson above the outer pavilions flirting with Art Nouveau. The attractive building that forms the angle between the theatre and Rupert Street was originally the Prince Rupert tavern, now a general store.

Internally the lively quality of the architecture

a prize for the eventual winner. An early proposal was the Mascot Theatre, but this was dropped, and the theatre opened as the Apollo on 21 February 1901 with an American musical, *The Belle of Bohemia*. For eight years musicals played at the theatre, and from 1909 to 1912 *The Follies* moved in. After 1913 musical comedy ceased, giving way to a mixed programme including Noël Coward's *Private Lives* in 1944 and *Seagulls Over Sorrento* in 1950; more recent successes include Alan Ayckbourn's *The Norman Conquests* and Keith Waterhouse's *Jeffrey Bernard Is Unwell*, starring Peter O'Toole.

RIGHT View from the dress-circle balcony looking at three tiers of serpentine-fronted boxes. High to the right, an ornamented ceiling pendentive supports a fine enriched oval, while to the left the tympanum relief dominates the proscenium arch.

APOLLO VICTORIA
THEATRE
WILTON ROAD

avid Atwell, in his influential work *Cathedrals of the Movies*, (1980) writes that 'as a work of architecture there is little doubt that the New Victoria is the most important cinema building to have been erected in Britain.' Designed by Ernest Wamsley Lewis and W. E. Trent in 1929, it is situated immediately to the east of Victoria Railway Station, slotting into a narrow row of buildings between the parallel streets of Wilton Road and Vauxhall Bridge Road. Thus the cinema has two impressive – though rather austere – Germanic Art Deco façades linked by a single foyer; the façades were originally transformed at night by seemingly endless concealed neon tubes. It was Lewis who actually produced the design, with Trent involved only as architect to Provincial Cinematograph Theatres, who owned the site. The concept is dramatic, the blank, streamlined horizontality of the main body of the building, faced in cast Portland stone, contrasting with the forceful verticality of the entrance bays. Two bas-relief panels by Newbury Abbot Trent, a sculptor better known for his memorials, are mounted either side of the Wilton Road entrance, accompanied by a small figure of Charlie Chaplin carved into the wall. A more eye-catching relief, by the same artist, paying homage to film, enhances the main staircase.

The auditorium is said to have been conceived as 'a mermaid's dream of heaven', a pale blue and green undersea wonderland of marine life beautifully enhanced by green, pink and blue lighting. The original stalactite lighting has long since disappeared, and part of the proscenium arch is in store, while a dolphin seems to have disappeared into the waves, along with lovely mermaid finials from the main staircase.

The New Victoria, as it was originally called, featured stage shows from the start. In 1933 the Royal Matinée for King George V was staged here, partly because of its convenient proximity to Buckingham Palace. Since then successes have included *The Sound of Music* with Petula Clark and *Camelot* with Richard Harris. Andrew Lloyd Webber's hit show *Starlight Express* opened here in 1984, and continued to attract good audiences into the new millennium.

Remarkable in the building industry, as Atwell points out, is the fact that the building was completed well within budget.

ABOVE Although the stalactite light fittings have gone, the surviving underwater details remain as a dramatic reminder of former days when elaborate lighting transformed the theatre from 'the colours of the dawn to the warm comfort of sunlight'.

ABOVE LEFT A beautiful stylized inhabitant of the 'Mermaid's Palace', W. E. Trent's fantastic wonderland, perches decorously in the theatre foyer.

BARBICAN THEATRE
SILK STREET

or 10 years after the Second World War the devastated area to the north of St Paul's Cathedral lay dormant, until in 1955 a joint London County Council and City of London rebuilding plan was conceived in an attempt to halt the City's depopulation. Previously the City Council had commissioned architects Chamberlin, Powell and Bon to design the Golden Lane Estate immediately to the north on a traffic-free grid, and so successful was this development that the same architects were selected to design the 35-acre Barbican development, again on a traffic-free grid – a colossal undertaking for a single practice. The Barbican concept would not be limited to the provision of housing: it was also planned to attract outsiders into the Corbusier-style complex. Accordingly, a theatre was built into the scheme as part of a wider vision encompassing an arts centre and the Museum of London. The Guildhall School of Music, which opened in 1997, is here, as is the City of London School for Girls.

On 2 March 1982 the Barbican Theatre was opened by the Queen as part of a larger arts complex, and in the same year the Royal Shakespeare Company became resident.

In the auditorium, arranged around a thrust stage, no bright colours are allowed to distract attention. Considerable consideration was given to sight lines through a clever arrangement of forward-rather than backward-stepping shallow balconies, with slips to left and right known in-house as 'the ashtrays'. At stalls level, continental seating – unbroken lengths of curving seating entered from the sides – is controlled by electromagnetic door locking: no latecomers! Much thought has also been given in the theatre to the comfort of, and easy access for, disabled persons.

Running along the back of the upper circle is the Sir Robert Stephens Room, dedicated to the memory of the great classical actor who joined the National Theatre in 1963, and died aged just 64 in 1996, having distinguished himself particularly in the leading Shakespearean roles.

ABOVE Modern, continental stalls seating.

BELOW Multifunctional megastructure buildings conceived in giant reinforced concrete presented an engineering solution to the City Council's brief.

CAMBRIDGE THEATRE
EARLHAM STREET

ABOVE These brass-faced doors are decorated with a lively, etched *moderne* geometric motif.

RIGHT One of three superb Germanic panels, depicting exercising nudes, which raise the quality of the circular entrance foyer.

pened in 1930, the Cambridge Theatre occupies the angle between Earlham Street and Mercer Street (formerly Great Earl Street and Little White Lion Street), one of the junctions that make up Seven Dials. Dominated by a central Doric column carrying six sundials, the pillar acting as the seventh, this is now a neat, clean, newly paved circus on the western edge of a revitalized Covent Garden. The present facsimile column, with its surrounding mixture of 18th- and 19th-century domestic and warehouse buildings, was unveiled by Queen Beatrix of the Netherlands on 29 June 1989, putting a stamp of approval on an area formerly notorious as a focus of the London underworld.

The land around Seven Dials was first developed in the 1690s, and so notorious did it become as a haunt of gangs and criminals that their gathering point, the original column, was removed in 1773. Over the ensuing 200 years little improved, and in the 19th century Monmouth Street, running north–south through the circus, was famous only for its unsavoury second- and third-hand clothes market. The area began to emerge from the murk when Charing Cross Road and Shaftesbury Avenue were created in the 1880s, and by the 1920s it was part of the working area of Covent Garden, centred on the market: not upmarket, but not slummy either.

The late 1920s and 1930s saw something of an explosion in theatre building in the West End, with, among others, the Adelphi, the Phoenix, the Fortune, the Piccadilly and the Carlton Haymarket opening their doors to the public for the first time. It is difficult to know exactly why the entrepreneur and speculator Bertie Meyer chose such an inconvenient triangular site on which to build a

ABOVE The contrast between the Doric Seven Dials column and the rather austere stone front of the theatre emphasizes the building's plainness. However, once theatre-goers step inside, they will experience Serge Ivan Chermayeff's fine interior.

theatre; as so often, the question of price springs to mind as a possible reason. The five-storey Portland-stone exterior of the Cambridge, with its chamfered entrance angle onto the circus, and long flank elevations relieved by mostly small windows, cannot be said to be exciting, but the interior has been touched by the hand of a master.

The building having been designed for Meyer by the successful practice of Wimperis, Simpson and Guthrie – a firm geared more to housing and office, rather than theatre, design – it was perhaps considered prudent to import a specialist to work on the interior. That specialist was a man of genius: Serge Ivan Chermayeff, a Russian who had come to England at the age of 10 and worked as director of the modern furnishings department at Waring & Gillow department store before establishing his own architectural practice in 1930. Later he was to design, with Erich Mendelsohn, what is probably the premier building of the modern movement in Britain: the De La Warr Pavilion at Bexhill-on-Sea, Sussex. In 1940 he emigrated to America. It is not known precisely how Meyer made the happy choice of his interior designer – the Cambridge was virtually Chermayeff's first commission in private practice – but the budding designer had doubtless made as many contacts as possible from his position at Waring & Gillow, and may already have been acquainted with Wimperis.

The foyer is graced by three panels of posed dancing and exercising nude figures, and the walls, once partly of marble, are now painted deep apricot, under a multilayered ceiling accommo-dating concealed lighting. A barrel-vaulted corridor sweeps round the back of the fan-shaped auditorium – which was originally painted pink, silver and blue and is now decorated in white and gold. Chermayeff brought into this theatre a clean-cut style, perhaps more familiar in Germany, which looked forward to the cinema architecture of the later 1930s. The elliptical shell-concrete ceiling is arranged in wide bands to provide a sophisticated scheme of concealed lighting, and the auditorium decoration is confined, for the most part, to *moderne* triangular patterning. Above the boxes are panels, one showing modern, gaunt buildings against a stylized sun, the other, the last rays of the setting sun with waves.

The theatre opened with Charlot's *Masquerade*, starring Beatrice Lillie, and established a pattern of musicals alternating with ballet and opera. *Half a Sixpence* with Tommy Steele was a huge success in the early 1960s, as was *Behind The Fridge* with Peter Cook and Dudley Moore in 1972.

COMEDY THEATRE
PANTON STREET

HISTORY

• 1881. Theatre designed by Thomas Verity for Alexander Henderson.

• Statutorily Listed Historic Building: Grade II.

OF SPECIAL INTEREST

• Eclectic classical façade on Panton Street.

• Three-tier cast-iron-columned horseshoe auditorium.

• Collection of memorabilia exhibited in the theatre.

• Seating capacity: 800.

ABOVE Detail of proscenium centrepiece.

anton Street takes its name from Colonel Thomas Panton, a friend of Charles II. Something of a blackguard, a swindler and a gambler, he managed to acquire an interest in some four acres of land between Leicester Square and Haymarket, legally owned by Robert Baker, a tailor. Also associated with the land was Sir Henry Oxenden, Baker's son-in-law, who contrived to establish joint ownership with Panton in 1669 following his inheritance of a life interest in the plot on Baker's death – carefully excluding Baker's descendants – and by the early 1670s building was under way. Two four-storey houses, still standing next to the theatre on its western side (although modernized externally around the mid-19th century), may well date from that 17th-century building activity. Also of particular interest in the street scene is the faience-fronted Tom Cribb pub, which perpetuates the name of the Gloucestershire-born coal porter who became a highly respected English bare-knuckle boxing champion in the 1800s.

Although much altered, the Comedy, which dates from 1881, remains one of the prettiest theatres in London. It was financed by owner J. H. Addison for manager and lessee Alexander Henderson, and designed by Thomas Verity, who had already built the Criterion Restaurant and Theatre on Piccadilly Circus in 1874. Verity's valuable early experience was gained with Captain Francis Fowke, working on what was to become the Victoria and Albert Museum (1865) and the Royal Albert Hall (1871). He died in 1891 at the age of just 54, leaving his son, F. T. Verity, to carry on his architectural practice.

RIGHT The outstanding quality of Thomas Verity's auditorium is captured in this view from the royal circle, looking down to the disused box at stage right.

The front of the theatre, on its corner site with Oxenden Street, is almost provincial in scale – reminiscent of, say, the Theatre Royal, Bristol, or the (now demolished) Theatre Royal, Leicester; of painted stone in an eclectic classical style, it originally housed a triple-arched entrance, but this has been replaced by grouped doorways in a channelled base under a mid-20th-century cantilevered canopy. The upper storeys are articulated by pilasters supporting an entablature and pediment. Between the pilasters at first-floor level are two architraved window openings and a blind central window occupied by a draped female figure carrying a flaming torch, each under an œil-de-bœuf.

Extensive alterations were made to the building in 1911, 1933 and again in 1955, but were generally restricted to the areas in and around the foyer and bars, leaving the three-tier iron-columned horseshoe-shaped auditorium virtually unaltered. The square architraved proscenium is flanked by shallow bow-fronted boxes, with palmette enrichment extending along the balcony fronts. In the decorative domed ceiling are the remains of a gas sunburner, a multi-flame burner which could be raised and lowered by winch from above; since the era of gaslight it has been replaced by a chandelier. Yellow and gold combined with modern lilac and gold have replaced the original white and gold decoration. The disused balcony bar, now a plant room, retains vestiges of its 19th-century decoration, with red panels divided by yellow ochre banding on a green dado.

The theatre houses a superb array of photographs, programmes and playbills, including a programme for the first production, in October 1881, of *The Mascotte*, starring Miss Violet Cameron. Among more recent actors and actresses to star at the Comedy are Susannah York, the late Sir Alec Guinness, Stephanie Cole, Dame Maggie Smith and Maureen Lipman. A plaque in the Royal Circle Bar records that the inaugural meeting of the Lords Taverners was held here on 3 July 1950.

LEFT A part elevational shot of the Comedy's comparatively small-scale façade, opening onto Panton Street.

CRITERION THEATRE
PICCADILLY CIRCUS

HISTORY

• From the 17th century to 1870, site occupied by the White Bear, a coaching inn.

• 1870. Site bought by Spiers and Pond, wine merchants. Thomas Verity wins architectural competition to build an entertainments complex.

• 1873. Criterion completed.

• 1879. Eastern extension added.

• Statutorily Listed Historic Building: Grade II*.

OF SPECIAL INTEREST

• The only basement theatre in London.

• Tilework and painting by Messrs Simpson and Son.

• Seating capacity: 592.

ABOVE This grinning fellow is one of the beautiful ensemble of polychromed tiles in the entrance foyer of the theatre.

reat coaching inns, such as the Bull and Mouth of St Martins-le-Grand in the City of London, and the Kings Head or the George Inn in Southwark, were an important element of the 17th- and 18th-century London scene, catering for the movements of considerable numbers of passengers each day through the capital. The White Bear, a 17th-century coaching inn, occupied a prime site on the south side of Piccadilly, with convenient access, via its large stableyard, to Jermyn Street at the rear. A popular inn, the White Bear survived beyond the coaching age to be demolished only in 1870. The purchasers of the site, wine merchants Spiers and Pond, held an architectural competition, won by Thomas Verity, architect of the nearby Comedy Theatre, for an entertainments complex incorporating a restaurant, pub and picture gallery with a concert and exhibition hall in the basement. The building was completed in 1873, an eastern extension was built in 1879, and a rear extension to Jermyn Street was added in 1885. The interiors were richly decorated in ornamental tile- and paintwork by Messrs Simpson and Son; the Long Bar and banqueting room remain virtually intact to this day.

The proposal to provide a theatre in the basement, replacing the concert and exhibition hall, was made part way through the contract, and the theatre was opened after the rest of the complex on 21 March 1874 – only to be closed by the Metropolitan Board of Works in 1882 on fire-safety grounds. Extensive improvements were made to the building, and the theatre reopened two years later. Further alterations were made in 1905, when the ground-floor buffet became the Marble Restaurant, with new doors to Piccadilly Circus; in 1908, when a new full-length iron and glass canopy was added to the front; and in 1921 and 1924, when part of the frontage was rebuilt and new floors added – all at the time when the distinguished architect and co-founder of the Art Workers' Guild Sir Reginald Blomfield was building to the west of the Criterion his grand entrance to Lower Regent Street in Portland stone and a Beaux-Arts classical manner. The east wing of the Criterion was demolished in the late 1980s and replaced by an office block designed by Renton Howard Wood Levine, with, on its angle into Haymarket, an eye-catching fountain dominated by the rearing *Horses of Helios*, sculpted in 1992 by Rudy Weller.

Looking across Piccadilly Circus from the north side, it is easy to lose the Criterion in what at first glance appears to be a monolithic block; but look again at the beautiful, delicate, eclectic classical stone front and be lifted above the welter of noise and mechanical turmoil. Eros has regrettably been moved on to a pedestrian area in front of the theatre, where he is cordoned off to prevent vandalism. Owing not a little to the Paris Opera House, the three main storeys of the Criterion are crowned, above a deep entablature, by a dormered mansard and pavilion roof. Although the front has been masked to its detriment by numerous layers of off-white paint, cherubs abound to raise the spirits. The restaurant and theatre each have separate entrances under pretty semi-circular glazed canopies. The theatre foyer is compact, but its painted and tiled decorative panels, which alternate with large plate-glass mirrors, give it a lively touch and provide an illusion of space. The coved ceiling depicts rather crude, ill-

LEFT The restrained frontage to Piccadilly Circus belies the full-blooded decoration in the small foyer and main staircase, with bright artwork (of questionable quality) by A. S. Coke and fine decorative tilework by Messrs Simpson and Sons.

BELOW The now painted stone façade to the Criterion complex is the finest surviving work of architect Thomas Verity, a delicate eclectic classical composition perhaps little noticed by many visitors to the attractions of Piccadilly Circus.

tempered cherubs, a muscular lyre player, and a musical maiden posed in a woodland garden. A single staircase drops down to the auditorium, which, although altered in 1884, retains its original horseshoe form of 1874, with two tiers of serpentine balconies supported on slender wreathed cast-iron columns. The balcony fronts are iron openwork, and the flat circular ceiling is ornamented with rococo relief panels. As the theatre is confined to the basement, no scenery can be flown – an openable prompt-side box provides for the movement of scenery – and no machinery

ABOVE The Criterion's delightful auditorium, with its decorative octagonal columns rising to support a flat ceiling, its serpentine open-fronted balcony and lyre-shaped upper circle, is the masterly creation of Thomas Verity.

RIGHT The quality of detail in the Criterion is no better highlighted than in this beautiful draped female figure adorning the staircase newel post.

was ever installed under the stage; this was no small limitation at a time when transformation scenes were extremely popular. Notwithstanding this inconvenience, the Criterion is a wonderful example of a Victorian multi-use complex, of which few survive; one other notable instance is Alexandra Palace at Muswell Hill (1875).

The theatre opened with a performance of *An American Lady*, a comedy written by the manager Henry J. Byron, but it was Sir Charles Wyndham's partner and later wife, actress Mary Moore, who was most prominently associated with the building from 1886 to 1931. Having managed the theatre since 1875, Charles Wyndham was lessee at his death in 1919. Being safely underground, the Criterion was used by the BBC as a studio during the Second World War, and since that time many successes have been performed here, including Joe Orton's *Loot* (1966), *The High Bid* with Eartha Kitt (1971) and *A Doll's House* with Claire Bloom (1973).

DOMINION THEATRE
TOTTENHAM COURT ROAD

HISTORY

• 1809. Erection of Henry Meux Horseshoe Brewery, demolished 1922.

• 1927. Dominion Theatres Ltd apply to London County Council for permission to build a theatre on the vacant site.

• 1929. Dominion Theatre opens on 3 October.

• 1930–81. Building used as a cinema.

• 1981. Building returns to use as theatre (and music venue).

• Statutorily Listed Historic Building: Grade II.

OF SPECIAL INTEREST

• The Dominion's place in the evolution of planning and decorative detailing.

• The building's lattice-girder and concrete construction.

• Seating capacity: 2,137.

ABOVE Ironwork of ever-changing geometric patterns adorns the double staircase out of the main foyer.

t Giles High Street, once the site of a gallows, and the junction of Oxford Street, New Oxford Street, Tottenham Court Road and Charing Cross Road are dominated by Centre Point, a controversial landmark office block designed by Richard Siefert and Partners in 1971. At the end of the 19th century the major buildings in the immediate vicinity were Henry Meux's Horseshoe Brewery, established in 1809, which occupied a large plot on the northeast corner of the crossroads and, to a lesser degree, the famous Oxford Music Hall, situated on the opposite, northwestern corner. The brewery was demolished in 1922 and the company, by then Friary Meux, was absorbed into Allied Breweries.

In 1926 the Casino Company proposed to build a theatre on the prominent corner site formerly occupied by the brewery – part of which had, since 1915, been occupied by the Court Cinema – but in late 1927, before a cost-effective scheme could be drawn up, the company was dissolved. Almost immediately Dominion Theatres Ltd, an offshoot of Moss Empires, submitted an application to the London County Council for permission to build a theatre with a capacity approaching 3,500. Their chosen architects were the brothers William and Thomas Ridley Milburn, who, from their base in Sunderland, had established a large practice in northeastern England and were already involved with Moss Empires in that region. In 1897, in partnership with Frank Matcham, they designed the Empire Palace, South Shields, on the site of Thornton's Theatre of Varieties. (Only a fragment of the Empire survives today.) A regular flow of theatre commissions followed, mainly around Sunderland and Newcastle upon Tyne, culminating in the neo-classical Dominion. This style option was inevitably judged by architectural pundits alongside the modern, streamlined, Art Deco super-cinemas of the period, such as the New Victoria, Westminster, by E. Wamsley Lewis and

RIGHT Vodka brewers Smirnoff once sponsored the Dominion Theatre, hence the theatrical mural in the dress-circle bar, now part of the historic fabric of the theatre.

RIGHT 'New Wave' theatre design with a breath of the super-cinema is here in the Portland-stone front of the Dominion. It is a pity the detail is partially obscured by a giant hoarding.

RIGHT The main staircase, with its fine ironwork, is elegantly lit by the original Art Deco glass light fittings.

OPPOSITE PAGE Original lighting abounds in the theatre, and the splendid central glass fitting dominates the grand space of William and Thomas Ridley Milburn's auditorium of 1929.

contrasting with an act-drop curtain of rainbow colours. Sumptuous lounges, retiring rooms and bars catered for the needs of the patrons. In December 1928 the *Architect and Building News* singled out the theatre as representing a high-water mark in modern construction, praising the ingenious use of a lattice-girder system to obviate the need for annoying columns inside the auditorium, but criticizing the use of outmoded decoration within the building.

The theatre opened on 3 October 1929, and in September 1930 an application to convert to cinema use was submitted and approved, allowing British International Pictures Ltd to put on performances continuously from 6 October that same year. In 1957 live shows were reintroduced into the theatre, interspersed with films. In 1958, Todd AO wide-screen projectors were installed, and on 21 April 1958 *South Pacific* opened for a record-breaking run of four and a half years, followed by *Cleopatra* in 1963. The Dominion reverted to continuous theatre use in 1981, since when it has provided a broad spectrum of mainly musical entertainment, from *Time* with Cliff Richard (1988), *Grease* (1993), *Scrooge* (1996) and *Notre-Dame de Paris* (2000) to *Swan Lake* (also 2000).

the Forum by A. Ernest Shennans, or theatres, including the Adelphi and the Strand, by Ernest Schaufelberg; and it was harshly treated by the comparison. It is not that the Milburns were in any way architectural Luddites; they were certainly not. They were, however, working through a transitional period in theatre design, when architects were slightly confused and tended to use 'old-fashioned' detail in 'forward-looking' buildings: thus they incorporated the up-to-date grand fanned plan, with sweeping ranks of curved seating, and the backward-looking ornamentation of much contemporary cinema building.

The design of the theatre was beautifully contrived by the architects to maximize the use of special lighting effects, both outside, on the narrow three-bay Portland-stone frontage, and within the building. The transition from the pavement to the grand entrance foyer is dramatic, confronting the entrant immediately with the fine marble and silvered double staircase rising up to the dress circle. The survival of the original suspended pink glass lighting fixtures in both the foyer and the auditorium is remarkable. Today burgundy and gold are the decorative colours in the auditorium, but on the opening night blue and silver presented a wonderful shimmering effect to the audience,

DONMAR WAREHOUSE
EARLHAM STREET

he Donmar Warehouse lies little more than a stone's throw to the east of Seven Dials and the Cambridge Theatre, at the northern extremity of Covent Garden, and occupies part of the upper floor of a former brewery warehouse dating from the mid-19th century. Along with the surrounding area, Earlham Street has been elegantly manicured since the 1970s when the fruit and vegetable market moved away. However, even as a pedestrian it is easy to bypass the theatre without registering its presence.

Extending for 23 sheer bays along the north side of the street, the three-storey, yellow stock brick building backs onto Short's Gardens, with the former Neal's Passage linking the two roads to form a triangular plot. As part of the overall upgrading of Covent Garden, the former warehouse was converted to a shopping mall in 1992, sacrificing its vaulted and cast-iron-columned industrial qualities for a contrived but friendly new interior. Within the development, the brewing flame is kept burning by the Freedom Brewing Company, dispensing pints of beer or lager brewed on the spot.

In the early 1920s the premises were in use as a pioneering colour film studio; later they were taken over for use as a banana warehouse. It was the meeting of the dedicated theatrical minds of Donald Albury and Margot Fonteyn that inspired the conversion to theatre use in 1960 – and the meeting of their forenames that gave it its title. Basic in every sense, in those early days the Donmar was mainly used for Royal Shakespeare Company rehearsals. From 1977 to 1981 the company used it as a studio theatre; then it decamped to the Barbican, and since 1981 the Warehouse has become a premier 'fringe' theatre.

Architects Renton Howard Wood Levine were responsible for the sensitive rehabilitation works, which combine simplicity with intimacy. Access to the theatre is via a single bay within the Earlham Street façade, into a narrow, white-painted brick entrance foyer and box office. Metal staircases with heavy wire balustrading ensure that the building's former life as a warehouse is not forgotten.

Above the foyer, the curving bars of the stalls and circles are formed around a communal lift shaft shared with the shops below. The auditorium is planned on the courtyard principle with a galleried balcony along three sides around a flexible protruding stage without wings or proscenium arch. Black-painted walls and bench seating covered in rust-tinted cloth ensure a sombre ambience, placing heavy reliance – as in so many modern theatres – on the plentiful lighting banks suspended above the acting area. This is a theatre that should be more widely known and appreciated.

ABOVE The entranceway to the box office and theatre retains the simple industrial qualities of the original warehouse.

LEFT Though basic in concept, the Donmar has blossomed into a premier 'fringe' theatre.

DRURY LANE –
THEATRE ROYAL
CATHERINE STREET

HISTORY

- 1636. Site of Monsieur Le Fèvre's riding academy.

- 1663. First theatre built, for Thomas Killigrew and the King's Company.

- 1674. Second theatre designed by Sir Christopher Wren for Thomas Killigrew.

- 1775. Third theatre designed by Robert Adam for David Garrick.

- 1790. Fourth theatre designed by Henry Holland to replace Robert Adam's following demolition.

- 1809. Fifth theatre built to designs of Benjamin Dean Wyatt after Holland's theatre burns down.

- 1922. Auditorium rebuilt by J. Emblin Walker, Edward Jones and Robert Cromie.

- Statutorily Listed Historic Building: Grade I.

OF SPECIAL INTEREST

- Extant fabric of Wyatt's rebuilding, including the entrance vestibule, rotunda, grand staircase and grand saloon.

- Samuel Beazley's cast-iron colonnade to Russell Street.

- Sculptures exhibited within the rotunda and vestibule.

- Memorial drinking fountain on Catherine Street elevation.

- Seating capacity: 2,188.

ABOVE The devil is in the detail, so it is said, and at the Theatre Royal fine detail abounds – a building of true joy, to be absorbed slowly.

RIGHT The elevation to Catherine Street. The portico was added over a decade after the rest of Benjamin Dean Wyatt's building was completed in 1809. This was in order to provide a more grand façade.

he Theatre Royal is situated on the cusp between fashionable Covent Garden to the west and the less attractive office and flat developments to the north and east. The main front opens not onto Drury Lane, as the name suggests, but onto Catherine Street, originally Brydges Street (1630s), but renamed after Catherine of Braganza. It overlooks a jolly run of 18th- and 19th-century domestic-scale buildings – now almost all restaurants – along with the Nell of Old Drury pub and the very fine Opera Tavern of 1879. To the north in Russell Street is Drury House, a typical late-20th-century office development, and across Crown Court is the Fortune Theatre, overshadowed by the sheer bulk and presence of its illustrious neighbour. Adjacent to the Theatre Royal at No. 6 Catherine Street is the Federation of Bakers, a five-storey red-brick and stone building of 1905, designed with nodding reference to Arts and Crafts architect C. F. A. Voysey.

Entertainment has taken place in Drury Lane since at least 1636, when Monsieur Le Fèvre, whose riding academy occupied the site of the present theatre, was authorized by the Lord Chamberlain, on behalf of Charles I, to convert his buildings for the use of a group of French actors. The *Survey of London* (Volume 35) records that 25 years later, in 1661, shareholders leased the site from the Earl of Bedford for the building of the Theatre Royal. In 1662 letters patent were conferred by Charles II on two actor–managers: Thomas Killigrew and his King's Company, and Sir William D'Avenant and the Duke's Company. These royal patents, licensing the recipients to set up theatre companies, in effect presented them with a theatrical monopoly. The Duke's Company was based at Lisle's Tennis Court, Lincoln's Inn; Killigrew built his own theatre the following year on the site of Le Fevre's riding academy, a building some 100 feet long by 50 feet wide, literally in the middle of the present theatre and approached by passageways from Brydges Street and Drury Lane. Forced to close down for the duration of the Great Plague (1664–5), the theatre reopened thereafter but was burnt down in 1672. For the reconstruction Killigrew engaged Sir Christopher Wren, who designed an intimate building that contributed much to the evolution of provincial theatres.

In the early 1740s a young actor named David Garrick was drawing huge crowds to Goodman's Fields, Whitechapel (where a theatre had been built in 1729, demolished and rebuilt in 1746) – to such an extent that the Theatre Royal was losing large numbers of regular patrons through a transfer of allegiance. Thus, of necessity, in May 1742 Garrick was engaged to appear at Drury Lane, where he dominated the stage for over three decades. In 1744 Garrick established his position with a brilliant performance as Macbeth, and in 1747 he entered into partnership with theatre manager James Lacy, obtaining a new patent from the Lord Chamberlain. He died in 1779, having retired from Drury Lane just three years earlier.

Until 1775 the Theatre Royal followed the pattern established at the Parisian Comédie Française, allowing the audience to occupy the sides of the stage. Intending to dispense with this inconvenience, Garrick commissioned the Scottish architect Robert Adam to redesign the theatre; in doing so, he cleverly introduced three tiers of boxes within the height of Wren's two. However, in 1790 the theatre was declared unsafe, and was demolished to make way for a new building designed by Henry Holland (who in 1789 had recased Althorp, the country home of the Spencer family, in grey mathematical tiles). Holland's other works include Spencer House in Piccadilly (1785–92); Cardiff Castle, which he reconstructed in the Gothic manner (1778); and the first Brighton Pavilion for the Prince Regent (1787).

On 24 February 1809 Holland's theatre was burnt down, and the competition to design the replacement building was won by Benjamin Dean Wyatt – at the time an inexperienced architect, though in 1813 he was to become Surveyor to Westminster Abbey, and after the end of the Napoleonic Wars would design a palace (never built) for the victorious Duke of Wellington. His design for Drury Lane, with its four circles of open boxes and two galleries, could accommodate an

ABOVE The auditorium of Walker, Jones and Cromie, 1922 is of high quality and incorporates elements of the original design.

audience of some 3,200, thus providing for a profitable operation; an eye on the economics of the project no doubt contributed to his success. The portico was added in 1820 to provide a grand façade to Catherine Street. The cast-iron colonnade to Russell Street, with its coupled, fluted Ionic columns and suspended lamp brackets, was added in 1831 by Samuel Beazley, who had rebuilt the Lyceum Theatre in 1816. The remainder of the 19th century saw only minor further amendments.

Although the auditorium was rebuilt in 1922 by J. Emblin Walker, Edward Jones and Robert Cromie, the interior is unique among London theatres in its retention of considerable elements of Wyatt's early 19th-century work. The beautifully proportioned Greek Doric vestibule gives access by three doors onto the central rotunda and flanking grand staircases to left and right. A statue of Shakespeare by John Cheere, brother of the more famous Sir Henry Cheere, is housed in the vestibule, while a second, along with statues of Michael Balfe (possibly by John Jones, 1846), David Garrick (sculptor unknown) and Edmund Kean (by John Edward Carew, 1833), is housed in the ground storey of the rotunda.

Little is known of the original colour scheme. Today the cream-painted rotunda soars upwards to its dome of pale ochre with green coffering, broken only by an elegant cantilevered stone gallery. On the gallery are busts of actor Ira Aldridge; Sir Johnson Forbes (better known as actor Forbes Robertson); Ivor Novello; and Samuel Whitbread by Joseph Nollekens, a sculptor of genius. Above the entrance is a lofty saloon decorated with paired Corinthian columns and pilasters; at either end is an apse, beyond one of which Wyatt placed a coffee room. In theatrical terms, the survival of Wyatt's work is without doubt of international significance.

The Empire style of the auditorium, decorated in pale blue-grey with Wedgwood blue and gold highlighting, accords well with Wyatt's surviving fabric. Three tiers of boxes are arranged in three bays either side of the rectangular proscenium with its imitation lapis lazuli frame. The sub-stage mechanics are very special, with a superb set of 'Asphaelia' machinery for raising and lowering sets and scenery, comprising four electric and two hydraulic bridges. The electric bridges, installed in 1898, can be raised to a height of seven feet or dropped a similar

LEFT The breathtaking rotunda of Benjamin Dean Wyatt can be seen at first-floor level. Corinthian columned screens under a deeply coffered dome with elegant ironwork comprise the centrepiece of one of the greatest survivals of theatre architecture in Britain.

BELOW This statue of William Shakespeare by John Cheere (1709–87), originally stood in the portico of the theatre, and now stands in the entrance hall.

SHAKESPEARE.

distance below stage level. The hydraulic bridges of 1896 can be tilted and will rise 12 feet above or drop eight feet below the stage. In 1908, 112 sets of counterweights were installed to replace the old pulley-based system of hemp line working.

On the Catherine Street elevation is a memorial drinking fountain of 1897, with a bust of impresario Sir Augustus Harris by Sir Thomas Brock, set in a round arched niche. The fountain was provided by public subscription through the Metropolitan Drinking Fountain and Cattle Trough Association.

Since Garrick's Macbeth of 1744 the Theatre Royal has hosted an astonishing array of productions, ranging from Shakespeare to pantomime and musicals. *The Merchant of Venice* was staged here in 1814, followed by *Macbeth* in 1835; nearly a century later Ivor Novello starred in *Henry V* (1930). Pantomimes include *Jack and the Beanstalk* (1899), *Cinderella* (1905) and *Aladdin* (1909); and the musicals *Show Boat*, starring Paul Robeson (1928), *The Dancing Years* (1939), *South Pacific* (1951) and *Camelot* (1964) each marked a theatrical milestone.

DUCHESS THEATRE
CATHERINE STREET

HISTORY

• 1929. Opened on 29 November, designed by Ewen S. Barr, with interior decoration by Marc Henri and Gaston Laverdet.

• 1935. Second interior scheme by Mary Wyndham-Lewis.

OF SPECIAL INTEREST

• Bas-reliefs by sculptor Maurice Lambert.

• Seating capacity: 476.

ABOVE Above the first-floor windows on the front elevation, the mono-grammed 'T. D.' panel is flanked on its right by a *fleur de lys* (heraldic lily).

RIGHT The south front of Castle Ashby House (Northampton-shire, 1630), attributed to Inigo Jones, could very well have provided the inspiration for the theatre façade. Embryonic it may be, but the architecture is firmly rooted in English Renaissance traditions.

atherine Street, opened in 1673 and named in honour of Charles II's Queen, Catherine of Braganza, whom diarist Samuel Pepys considered 'mighty pretty', extended south to the Strand until the opening of Aldwych in 1905. Until 1974 its northern end fed into the organized conglomeration of wagons, carts, containers and porters that was Covent Garden Market, prior to the market moving in that year to modern accommodation at Nine Elms. Since then, the shops and pubs that catered for the contrasting needs of market and theatre-goers alike have been transformed almost en masse into the boutiques and bistros that crowd around the Duchess.

In the early 1920s the site was owned by William Clarkson, a theatrical costumier, who had ambitions to build his own theatre. His vision came to nought, however, because of problems he encountered with the law of Ancient Lights, specifically the illegal obstruction of one's neighbour's daylight that would result

RIGHT View of auditorium
showing prompt-side
bas-relief panel by
Maurice Lambert.

from the building planned. Finally he gave up and sold the plot to West End and Country Theatres Ltd, which leased it on to Arthur Gibbons, a promoter whose choice of architect Ewen S. Barr was inspired.

Barr must have spent many hours at his drawing board before the persistent problem that had defeated Clarkson was finally solved. He would sink the stalls deep into the ground, extending back under the foyer and what is now the dress-circle bar, which in turn would be formed into the underside of the dress circle. The resultant low-rise design overcame the daylight obstacle, and a small but attractive theatre was born. Interestingly, at almost the same time that Barr was designing for Gibbons, he was looking to the future and producing, with T. R. Sommerford, the interiors of four early atmospheric London Astoria cinemas.

Externally, the embryonic 'Elizabethan' Portland-stone frontage, with its three shallow canted bay windows and simplified decorative motifs, forms a loose group with the Strand Theatre on the opposite side of the road, and the Theatre Royal, Drury Lane, to the north. Originally, the equally simple Art Deco interior with dished, domed ceiling was enlivened by a sensitive colour scheme in blue, silver and mauve by Marc Henri and Gaston Laverdet, later to be redesigned by Mary Wyndham-Lewis, wife of the playwright J. B. Priestley. Sadly, the only survivals of this decoration in today's partially artexed and cream-painted auditorium are two rather special bas-reliefs, which were designed by the young sculptor Maurice Lambert, flanking the proscenium arch.

The Duchess opened on 25 November 1929; among its successes are J. B. Priestley's *Laburnum Grove*, which ran for 335 performances in 1933, and Emlyn Williams's *The Corn Is Green*, which ran for 395 performances in 1938. More recently, the highly successful *Oh! Calcutta* was transferred here from the Royalty, followed in 1986 by *No Sex Please – We're British*, which completed a run of 6,671 performances at the Duchess, having transferred from the Garrick.

DUKE OF YORK'S THEATRE

ST MARTIN'S LANE

ABOVE A detail from the elegant arabesque decoration that ornaments the upper-circle balcony front.

RIGHT The theatre's main entrance opens onto St Martin's Lane. The first-floor Ionic columned loggia fronts the dress-circle bar.

hould the spirit of the 2nd Earl of Salisbury hover briefly above St Martin's Lane, Cecil Court and St Martin's Court, he would see little evidence of the fashionable enclave he developed in the first decades of the 17th century. He would, however, see Burleigh Mansions (once the home of actress Ellen Terry), dated 1892, with its fine, well-preserved shop fronts, immediately north of the Duke of York's. Further north he would see a symmetrical five-storey red-brick chamber block of 1899, incorporating The Salisbury public house, which perpetuates the old Earl's memory, adjacent to the Albery Theatre. Architecturally the pub is one of the finest in the West End, having an excellent collection of frosted and cut glass, rich mahogany fittings and Art Nouveau candelabra. The Earl would also see with great pleasure a building of considerable moment to the south of the pub: the Duke of York's Theatre (originally the Trafalgar Square Theatre), designed by Walter Emden and opened on 10 September 1892, two years after the Garrick Theatre in Charing Cross Road, which Emden produced in partnership with C. J. Phipps.

Although Emden designed only eight theatres from scratch, thus falling well short of the numbers produced by Frank Matcham, Phipps, W. G. R. Sprague and Bertie Crewe, the Duke of York's, which he built for Frank Wyatt and Violet Melnotte, is a building of considerable quality and a tribute to the architect's planning skills, albeit enhanced a little by contrast with its modern neighbours. The symmetrical front, in restrained later classical style, is four storeys high and faced in pale green painted brickwork with cream stucco detail. The arcaded and channelled stucco ground storey is painted battleship grey. At first-floor level, above a much altered canopy, is a balustraded loggia with Ionic

ABOVE LEFT Neo-classical stucco reliefs sit above the proscenium arch in the Louis XVI interior.

ABOVE RIGHT Three tiers of single boxes form the proscenium arch with flanking double boxes at dress- and upper-circle levels.

columns fronting the upper-circle bar; the elevation is unified by the judicious use of Ionic pilasters, decorative entablatures and a crowning cornice. High-quality original wrought-iron gates close off access ways to the north and south.

Internally, a strangely sub-17th-century entrance vestibule opens into a square foyer, coloured pink between white and gold fluted Corinthian pilasters above a panelled dado. A plaque records major alterations to the building carried out in 1980 by architects Jaques, Muir and Partners for the owners Capital Radio, who used part of it as a studio. The theatre was again refurbished in 1999, in a process of redecoration with minor alterations to enhance the whole interior.

The narrowness of the site, and the headaches it must have given the architects, are evident in the picturesque but compressed three-tier cream, gold and pink Louis XVI-style auditorium, and the full-width proscenium arch. Dressing rooms are housed in a separate block, linked to the rear of the main building. Balcony fronts to the royal and upper circles are quite lavishly decorated with arabesque and

grotesque ornamentation, while simple palm groups are used above a reeded and ribboned band on the front of the gallery, which has remained unrestored since the building was taken over by Capital Radio. An elegant ribbed and coffered dome, ornamented with acanthus, masks and winged figures, completes the ensemble. The upper-circle bar perpetuates the auditorium's decorative theme with some success, but the remaining bars are of little moment. A plaque in the upper-circle bar records a mass meeting of actors and actresses on 1 December 1929, and its resolution to form the British Actors' Equity Association.

Timber sub-stage machinery was probably installed in 1905 for a performance of *Peter Pan* with Charlie Chaplin, but regrettably this has been virtually demolished. Under the fly floor a cyclorama track was in situ in the early 1970s.

The theatre's opening production starred Decima Moore in *The Wedding Eve*, and Marie Tempest performed here in *The Marriage of Kitty* in 1902. Much later, one of the theatre's greatest successes came in the 1980s with a production of *Stepping Out* by Richard Harris, which ran for well over two years.

FORTUNE THEATRE
RUSSELL STREET

ABOVE This pretty
beaten copper
pay-box is
located in the
small, square
marble foyer.

RIGHT Once
decorated with
murals, the
auditorium is
extremely
compact. There
are no stage
boxes and the
flat-fronted dress
circle is very close
to the action on a
stage that is very
small by West
End standards.

he year 1930 would see the architect Ernest Schaufelberg commissioned to rebuild the Adelphi Theatre in the Strand as a grand exercise in a mature Art Deco style; in 1922–4, at the Fortune, he was producing for impresario Lawrence Cowen a minor gem in which the exterior embodies the fundamentals of Cubism while at the same time opening the door to Art Deco and modernism. The Fortune was the first theatre to be built in London after the First World War, and as a forward-looking piece of architecture it should be judged in the context of Sprague's St Martin's (1916) and Verity and Beverley's Carlton Haymarket (1927), the second post-war London Theatre.

In concept, the cream, bush-hammered reinforced concrete front, on the west angle with Crown Court, is essentially Cubist, a style originating in the art of Braque and Picasso and evolving into the architecture of the Modern Movement. Windows with geometric glazing bars are carefully placed on the

asymmetrical façade, contrasting with the long, colonnaded flank elevation of the Theatre Royal, Drury Lane, on the opposite side of the road. Two pairs of elaborately glazed Art Deco entrance doors survive in the ground storey, lightened by banding with stylized waves and decorated in maroon, black and dull gold. High on the façade is a gilded, seated nude female figure, probably representing the Roman goddess Fortuna, by M. H. Crichton. A modern canopy extends the width of the frontage.

On this very small site Schaufelberg was required to absorb into his theatre the long corridor entrance to the red-brick and stone Church of Scotland building to the rear – that is, fronting onto Crown Court. A stone-pedimented Doric doorcase gives access from Russell Street, and in a clever piece of planning the corridor is not discernible from within the theatre. The small, square foyer is lined with red and grey marble, housing on one side a very pretty original beaten copper pay-box; on the other side, staircases give access to the stalls and circle levels.

The blue-grey and gold auditorium is simple but intimate, the chevron-panelled balcony fronts being, by necessity, brought unusually well forward. Two tiers of boxes are emphasized by a drop-beam on the line of the dress-circle front, and triple domes extending across the proscenium arch.

The theatre opened on 8 November 1924 with *Sinners*, a play written by the theatre's owner, Cowen, followed by *On Approval* (1927) and *Cape Forlorn* (1930), both by Frederick Lonsdale, under the managership of Tom Walls. Sybil Thorndike, Dirk Bogarde, Kenneth More, and Michael Flanders and Donald Swann have all appeared on this small stage. *Beyond The Fringe* with Peter Cook and Dudley Moore ran here for four years in the early 1960s, and 30 years later Susan Hill's *The Woman In Black* would run for two years.

'There is a tide in the affairs of men.
Which, taken at the flood, leads on to fortune.'
Brass plaque in theatre foyer

GARRICK THEATRE
CHARING CROSS ROAD

HISTORY

• Named after the great 18th-century actor David Garrick.

• 1889. Designed for W. S. Gilbert by Walter Emden and C. J. Phipps.

• Statutorily Listed Historic Building: Grade II*.

OF SPECIAL INTEREST

• The Bath and Portland stone screen wall to Charing Cross Road.

• Interior, including foyer, auditorium and upper-circle bar.

• Good original entrance doors.

• Seating capacity: 724.

ABOVE A portrait of a colleague, or a self-portrait? Who knows, but such details make a careful inspection of the Garrick Theatre exceedingly rewarding.

RIGHT Overlooking the flank elevation to the National Portrait Gallery, the main front of the theatre is an exercise in eclectic classicism. The six-bay Corinthian colonnaded loggia at first-floor level provides the ideal spot to enjoy a drink during the interval.

ehind the stalls bar there hangs a copy of probably the best-known portrait of the great 18th-century actor David Garrick, depicted by Thomas Gainsborough with a bust of Shakespeare. In the National Portrait Gallery, a stone's throw away to the south of the theatre, hangs a lesser-known work by Sir Joshua Reynolds. In the latter, Garrick, looking well-rounded and avuncular, sits in the garden of his country house by the Thames at Hampton with his devoted wife, Eva (née Violetti) whom he married in 1749 at the age of 32. However, to capture the elusive, multifaceted character of probably the greatest actor of his time, in whose honour the theatre was named, it is necessary to look to Louis-François Roubiliac's plaster bust, also in the keeping of the National Portrait Gallery. Here it is possible to glimpse the 'moving brow and penetrating eye' and to sense the 'shifting passions' born of the energy and versatility that marked Garrick out from his contemporaries.

The southern end of Charing Cross Road was created during the mid-1880s by widening what was then Castle Street, and by demolishing a considerable number of small buildings in order to achieve the sweep round the back of the National Gallery into Trafalgar Square. A particularly large and dominating victim of the demolitions was St Martin's Workhouse, which stood on the site now occupied by the National Portrait Gallery.

Always astute, it was W. S. Gilbert (of Gilbert and Sullivan fame) who, notwithstanding the irregular shape of the site, leased it from the Metropolitan Board of Works, commissioning architect Walter Emden to design a theatre for actor–manager John Hare. It appears to have been Emden who was responsible

for the basic layout of the building, but, possibly as a result of his recent successful work on the equally irregular Lyric Theatre site in Shaftesbury Avenue, it was C. J. Phipps who was brought in to 'run the job'.

The auditorium is orientated north–south, and runs parallel to Charing Cross Road behind an articulated screen wall, the main entrance vestibule and foyer being at the northern end. Adjacent to the theatre entrance, now under a modern glazed canopy, is a wide, gated access, allowing the pit and gallery audience to queue away from the public thoroughfare. *The Builder* magazine, marking the opening of

the theatre on 24 April 1889, remarked that 'Architectural art in the true sense seems to have been kept at a safe distance,' but this was perhaps somewhat unfair; certainly the balanced, now partially painted, Bath stone façade set on a rusticated and channelled Portland-stone podium is an eclectic classical composition of considerable merit.

Above the main entrance is a Corinthian colonnade and open loggia now fronting the upper-circle bar, while the screen wall further south is enriched by pilastered semi-circular headed bays.

The auditorium, in a free Italian Renaissance style, retains most of its original features and is

LEFT Under a superb domed ceiling, the figured dress- and upper-circle balcony fronts and simplified gallery front, so carefully planned by Phipps, allow a friendly atmosphere without becoming overly intimate.

BELOW This copy of Thomas Gainsborough's fine portrait of David Garrick, with a bust of Shakespeare, hangs behind the stalls bar. The original painting was lost.

arranged on a 'U' plan. The decoration appears to adhere fairly closely to the original colours of cream and gold, with the accent on a generous amount of gold highlighting. The walls to the rear of the auditorium are hung in deep red, vertically striped paper, probably shades darker than would originally have been in place, but effective nevertheless. The quality of the decoration extends to the foyer, with its Adamesque plasterwork, and to the upper-circle bar, likewise decorated in a mid-18th-century manner.

John Hare appeared with Forbes-Robertson in the theatre's first production, Pinero's *The Profligate*, and went on to make regular appearances with considerable success. Following Hare's retirement in 1896, the theatre came under the management of Harry Brickwell and then passed into the hands of Arthur Bourchier, who immortalized his name by refusing access to *The Times*' drama critic in 1903. In 1934 an attempt to revive music hall came to nothing, but the following year *Love on the Dole*, with Wendy Hiller, revived the theatre's fortunes. In the years after the Second World War many great theatrical names were associated with the Garrick, including Jack Buchanan, Beatrice Lillie, Laurence Olivier, Rita Tushingham and Brian Rix.

GIELGUD THEATRE
SHAFTESBURY AVENUE

HISTORY

• 1906. Designed for Jack Jacobus and Sydney Marler by W. G. R. Sprague and named the Hicks Theatre.

• 1909. Name changed to the Globe on Hicks's withdrawal.

• 1994. Name changed again in honour of Sir John Gielgud.

• Statutorily Listed Historic Building: Grade II.

OF SPECIAL INTEREST

• The elevational treatment of the block including the Queen's Theatre.

• The double-height circular foyer.

• Seating capacity: 889.

ABOVE This extremely ornate centrepiece sits above the proscenium arch.

hen Shaftesbury Avenue was created in the West End redevelopments of the 1880s, much of it cut through built-up areas which were demolished to make way for it. However, with a view to preserving the character of Soho, from Greek Street westwards towards Regent Street it followed the line of the former King Street and Richmond Street, these older thoroughfares being widened on their south side to accommodate the new avenue. Thereafter, the short stretch between Rupert Street and Piccadilly Circus broke completely new ground. At the very end of the old section, on the brink of the new, stands the Gielgud, formerly the Globe Theatre.

The origins of the Gielgud lie with a boot- and shoe-maker, Jack Jacobus, whose premises were in Shaftesbury Avenue, and an estate agent, Sydney Marler. In 1904 these two, in partnership, acquired a lease on the block of buildings bounded by Rupert Street, Wardour Street and Winnett Street, with a view to erecting two theatres and also expanding Jacobus's business. They commissioned the architect W. G. R. Sprague to produce a master plan for the site, which he did by placing a theatre at each main angle, with the expanded boot and shoe holding between the two, fronting onto Shaftesbury Avenue. Jacobus and Marler were joined in their venture by the actor Seymour Hicks, after whom one of the playhouses was named. The Hicks Theatre, on the southeast angle, opened on 27 December 1906, and the Queen's, on the southwest angle, almost a year later on 8 October 1907. Hicks, however, quickly lost interest and pulled out; as a consequence the name of the first theatre changed in 1909 to the Globe. In 1994 the reconstructed 'Shakespeare's Globe' opened on Bankside

RIGHT Dynamic free baroque decoration is beautifully utilized by W. G. R. Sprague. His use of subtle variations in the geometry of the auditorium demonstrates the architect's vision and three-dimensional design ability.

notable roles on film, including an Oscar-winning performance as Hobson, Dudley Moore's butler in the comedy *Arthur*.

Sprague's group originally presented a lively, almost symmetrical Portland-stone faced composition to Shaftesbury Avenue; but it lasted only until 1940, when the Queen's was badly damaged by enemy bombing. Its undamaged companion, however, continues to sit extremely comfortably with the colourful street-market and strip-bar world of Rupert Street. Its design in a free baroque style is typical of Sprague's work, cleverly turning the corner into Rupert Street using a bowed angle, emphasized by giant Ionic columns supporting a buttressed circular tower and dome. High-level œil-de-bœuf windows and balustrading unify the two main elevations; a subordinate 10-bay flank elevation extends along Rupert Street faced in red brick.

The circular entrance foyer comprises a very attractive, airy, double-height cream and gold space reminiscent of the smoking gallery at the Aldwych Theatre (also designed by Sprague), here enhanced by Ionic pilasters and putti spandrels under a domed ceiling. The auditorium, carrying through this circular theme, is decorated in Louis XIV style, now coloured a pinky peach. The side walls to the two cantilevered balconies are dressed with paired Ionic columns, partly buried within the wall, between which roundels are placed at dress-circle level, depicting scenes including Pan playing for dancing cherubs. At the rear of the dress circle the former grand saloon, now the bar, is an extension of the overall decorative scheme. On either side of the proscenium two tiers of boxes are flanked by pedestalled Corinthian pilasters, and the 12-panel circular domed ceiling is ornamented by swags of flowers.

Of the timber stage machinery that dates from the building of the theatre, enough survives of the original four bridges, slotes and traps to illustrate its fine quality.

The theatre opened with a production of *The Beauty of Bath*, starring Seymour Hicks and Ellaline Terriss; this was followed by successes penned by Somerset Maugham, Noël Coward and Ivor Novello. In 1939 John Gielgud starred in Oscar Wilde's *The Importance of Being Earnest*, and from 1949 he appeared in Christopher Fry's *The Lady's Not For Burning*, *Nude With Violin* and *The Potting Shed*. Peter Hall's production of *Hamlet* honoured the renaming of the theatre in 1994. In 2000 the Gielgud became a Really Useful Theatre when Lord Lloyd Webber and NatWest Equity purchased the building, and Kathleen Turner opened in *The Graduate*.

ABOVE The Gielgud, with its circular Portland-stone tower under a stone dome, makes an unashamedly bold statement on the corner of Rupert Street. This would have appealed greatly to speculators Jack Jacobus and Sydney Marler, in search of full houses and hefty profits.

within the shadow of the Tate Modern Gallery, and the older theatre was renamed in honour of the man who was one of the 20th century's greatest British actors.

Sir John Gielgud, who died on 21 May 2000 aged 96, was the son of a stockbroker father and a mother who was related to the great 19th-century actress Ellen Terry. A master of classical roles, once referred to by the late Sir Alec Guinness as 'a silver trumpet muffled in silk', he starred in a number of successful productions at the Globe. Equally at ease on stage and screen, Gielgud played many

HAYMARKET –
THEATRE ROYAL
HAYMARKET

ABOVE
This wonderful cluster of lanterns highlights the superb quality of detail to be found in theatre buildings, so often written off as frivolous or trifling by 'serious' commentators.

OPPOSITE Part-elevational detail of architect John Nash's exemplary neo-classical front to the Theatre Royal of 1820–21. The Corinthian columned portico extends out over the pavement.

tanding under the canopy of Her Majesty's Theatre to look across the Haymarket, it is extremely difficult to compose a picture in one's mind's eye of the immediate area in 1513, when John Norris willed to his wife, Christian, his croft along with an enclosed three-acre toft. Picturesque it probably was not, close to an area where the expanding City of London would meet a developing City of Westminster; but this was the field upon which the Theatre Royal would eventually be built. In 1575 the land was occupied by the widow Golightly, and in 1610 the Earl of Northampton was building stables on it. Around 1614 the Earl of Suffolk bought the stables along with nearby Northampton House and changed their name. By the end of the 17th century Suffolk Street and its environs were laid out, and handsome, 'well-inhabited' houses began to appear.

In 1720 John Potter, a local carpenter, built the New French Theatre on the site of the King's Head, an inn fronting the Haymarket, and a gun shop in Suffolk Street to its rear, demolishing both to make way for the playhouse. Situated in the northwest angle of John Norris's toft, it lay to the north of the modern theatre, and it was not until about 1730 that it became known as The Little Theatre in the Haymarket. Officially closed in 1737 under the Licensing Act of George II, the theatre managed by various ingenious, not to say nefarious, means to keep going. In 1767, a royal patent was granted permitting the house to 'exhibit plays' between May and September in an enlarged and improved building renamed the Theatre Royal – thus breaking the grip on the theatrical profession held by Drury Lane and Covent Garden, the only two other playhouses licensed by royal patent. Eventually, however, with the manager George Colman failing to run the theatre efficiently from prison, where he was in residence for debt, the building was closed around 1818–19, and lost in subsequent conversion works around 1819–20.

The decline and demise of the theatre may to some extent be accounted for by the general dilapidation of its surroundings, and it was reborn when architect John Nash produced a regeneration scheme aimed at revitalizing Suffolk Street and its immediate neighbourhood in the early 1820s. Talented architects such as J. P. Gandy-Deering, one of three eminent architect brothers, and William Wilkins, who designed the National Gallery in 1834, built here – all under the strict design control of Nash, who himself provided a number of houses, including No. 6 Suffolk Street, the Gallery of the Royal Society of British Artists (restored in 1979).

As part of his grand plan Nash encouraged the rebuilding of the theatre as a focal point on the axis of Charles II Street, and to this end he proposed a deep, giant pedimented, six-columned Corinthian portico with five arched doorways giving access to the pit, boxes, galleries and box office. This configuration echoed the flat-roofed four-columned portico of the earlier building. Above the proposed portico, a sheer attic wall pierced only by a recessed panel of nine radial glazed oculi would be provided. Like the front, the Suffolk Street elevation is stuccoed and distinctly domestic in character. Internally the auditorium was almost square, with two levels of boxes extending around three sides and enclosing the pit. Access corridors ran behind the boxes from an entrance lobby.

The theatre reopened on 4 July 1821 under the management of David

Morris, George Colman's brother-in-law, with a production of Richard Brinsley Sheridan's *The Rivals*. In 1843 'extensive alterations' were made when the stage was pushed back to allow the introduction of orchestra stalls, and pit seats were abolished to be replaced by the more expensive stalls.

Squire Bancroft, who had managed the Scala in Charlotte Street from 1871, took over at the Haymarket in 1879, immediately initiating a rebuilding programme and commissioning architect C. J. Phipps to remodel the interior, modernizing it and bringing it up to date with a picture-frame proscenium and a reseated auditorium. Decorative plasterwork was executed by George Jackson and Sons, a firm that retained in its workshops until the late 20th century a wonderful collection of 18th-century moulds.

Herbert Beerbohm Tree, one of the last great actor–managers, ran the theatre from 1888 until he moved to Her Majesty's in 1896. In October that same year Frederick Harrison and Cyril Maude, who moved to the Playhouse in 1907, took over and in 1904 set out to modernize yet again, engaging architects Charles Stanley Peach and S. D. Adshead to

carry out the work – an odd choice, as Peach's reputation was built on electricity generating stations and his design for the Centre Court buildings at Wimbledon. The work was confined in the main to the auditorium, where a modern structural frame replaced the perhaps less stable existing fabric. The result is a stunning essay in elegant Louis XVI decoration, surpassed nowhere in London.

In a deep cellar behind the proscenium arch, 19th-century timber stage machinery still survives today; three bridges remain in situ with original sliders, a rarity indeed. Between 1915 and 1939 a three-piece sliding stage was installed using boat trucks. Regrettably, the thunder run was removed in 1970 to accommodate a new counterweight system.

A plaque on the back of the building records that the first performances of Oscar Wilde's *A Woman of No Importance* (1893) and *An Ideal Husband* (1895) took place here.

Historically of tremendous importance, this theatre has been the subject of books and lectures on all of its aspects; and doubtless one day, when the fabric becomes unsteady through age, the archaeologists will have their say, too.

RIGHT The survival of the great central chandelier in the auditorium is a tribute to the owners and managers who have cared about this theatre's wonderful interior over the years.

HER MAJESTY'S THEATRE

HAYMARKET

ABOVE Ram's-head ornamentation extends the decorative quality of the theatre into its furnishings.

OPPOSITE The French Renaissance design of Her Majesty's was considered imposing and a welcome addition to London's theatre world by *The Times* in 1897. At night, subtle lighting emphasizes the skill with which architect C. J. Phipps piled up the elevations to terminate in his square dome.

oday a seemingly endless stream of traffic pours down Haymarket, as it drops southwards from Piccadilly Circus to Trafalgar Square, but on 9 April 1705, when the first theatre on the site was opened, the scene was vastly different. Since the mid-17th century a hay and straw market had flourished here to such an extent that it was considered by many to be a public nuisance; but it was on Crown land, and rather than order its closure, in 1663 King Charles II granted to the Earl of St Albans the additional right to hold a twice-weekly cattle market, probably exacerbating the existing nuisance. It was not until 1830 that the trade in hay, straw and cattle was removed to Cumberland Market to the east of Regents Park, by which time some 30,000 loads were being turned over annually.

And so it must have been a rather agricultural environment that John Vanbrugh chose in 1703 as the location for a theatre he was to design for Thomas Betterton's company of actors, backed by 'thirty Persons of Quality', to be known as the Queen's Theatre. Vanbrugh, who was just embarking on his new career as an architect, having spent his early life soldiering, was also a playwright and an opportunist, and he decided with Betterton to take advantage of disagreement and bad management at the Theatre Royal, Drury Lane. With fellow playwright William Congreve, Vanbrugh opened with Greber's opera, *The Loves of Ergasto*. However, two problems rapidly became apparent: first, Vanbrugh's grasp of financial matters was somewhat shaky; and second, his natural urge to design in the grand manner resulted, as actor and dramatist Colley Cibber famously remarked, 'in quality and convenience being sacrificed for a vast triumphal Piece of Architecture'. Over the ensuing years debt is a recurring theme in the theatre's history until, on 17 June 1789, the building (by now known as the King's Theatre, having been renamed on the accession of George I), was totally destroyed by fire, allegedly set by one Carnivalli, a disgruntled former employee.

Within two years, Michael Novosielski, a trustee of the earlier theatre, reconstructed the building on a scale that made it the second largest opera house in Europe, surpassed only by La Scala, Milan. Presenting opera and ballet, it opened on 26 March 1791, again as the King's Theatre; it was here that Mozart's *Così fan Tutte* was first produced in London (1811), followed in 1812 by *The Magic Flute*. To ensure that it remained fashionable, John Nash collaborated in 1816 with George Repton, son of the more famous Humphrey Repton, to remodel the building, providing the attractive Royal Opera Arcade at its western end and colonnading the remaining sides. A golden age of opera followed the reconstruction, until an apparently faithful audience drifted away to the rising Royal Opera House in Covent Garden, and the renamed Her Majesty's Theatre (1837) was forced to close in 1852. After a period of four years the theatre reopened, only to be ravaged by fire on 6 December 1867. Again, in 1869, the theatre was rebuilt within the skeletal walls that survived the fire by Charles Lee, an architect who had worked in the office of John Nash. He provided an auditorium of a quality commensurate with the design genius of his mentor, seating up to 2,500, and with a large stage, the whole incorporating a much improved fireproof construction. However, financial problems meant that the

RIGHT The dress-circle bar, decorated in cream and gold, overlooking the main staircase through an open arcaded screen. Four dark portraits hang on the staircase, including Miss Dorothy Baird as Trilby and Tchernicheva in *The Good Humoured Ladies.*

theatre failed to open until 1875, when it was used for religious meetings; later it returned to staging opera, and also pantomime, until in 1890 it again closed in debt. The contents were auctioned, and the building – apart from the Royal Opera Arcade – demolished.

Over the next five years various designs were considered for building on the vacant site, and in 1895 C. J. Phipps, one of the most prolific of theatre architects, whose golden rule was 'there must not be a bad seat in the house', was commissioned to rebuild the theatre for the great actor–manager Herbert Beerbohm Tree. In the present entrance foyer is a green marble commemoration stone laid by Maud Beerbohm Tree on 16 July 1896. The

interior decoration was to be designed by Romaine Walker, Tree's consulting architect.

Phipps devised the present stone-faced theatre, smaller than its predecessor, on the northern part of the site in a French Renaissance style of four main storeys under attics and a large pavilion roof, crowned by a fine square dome. The southern part of the site would be occupied by the Carlton Hotel and Restaurant, which was to be demolished in 1957 to make way for New Zealand House, a predominantly glass building by Robert Matthew, Johnson-Marshall and Partners erected in 1963 and typical of its age. C. J. Phipps did not live to see his theatre completed, dying in 1897, but he must have known that this last work would be one of his finest

ABOVE The theatre's scagliola proscenium has been temporarily masked by an elaborate frame for the long-running production of *The Phantom of the Opera*, with memorable music by Andrew Lloyd Webber and Richard Stilgoe. This intrusion, however, does little to detract from Romaine Walker's wonderful auditorium of 1897.

achievements. Today Her Majesty's Theatre makes an important contribution to a street of mixed architectural fortunes. From its northern approach – Piccadilly Circus – it is sad to see the dome, designed to emphasize the presence of the building, overshadowed by the looming, now slightly dour backdrop of New Zealand House; but in the heady post-war 1950s, this unfortunate juxtaposition would have raised few eyebrows.

Internally the auditorium, with its fanned stalls seating, cantilevered balconies and gallery, has a refined French neo-classical feel. The scagliola proscenium is flanked by three-tier boxes set between Corinthian columns. The original colours of white and gold have been replaced by a warmer green and apricot with gold highlighting. The flat stage conceals the finest set of English wooden stage machinery in London, including, at fly-floor level, an unusually complete thunder run. Beerbohm Tree, for his part, took up residence in the specially fitted-out dome, living there until his death in 1917.

Among the many notable presentations at the theatre were Oscar Asche's *Chu Chin Chow*, which ran for 2,238 performances in 1916; Noël Coward's *Bitter Sweet* (697 performances) in 1929; *Fiddler on the Roof* (2,030 performances) in 1967; *West Side Story* in 1984; and the superb *Phantom of the Opera*, which opened on 9 October 1986 and was still showing into the new millennium.

LONDON COLISEUM

ST MARTIN'S LANE

HISTORY

• 1902–4. Theatre designed and built by architect Frank Matcham for Oswald Stoll.

• Statutorily Listed Historic Building: Grade II*.

OF SPECIAL INTEREST

• Matcham's little-altered masterpiece, a superb variety theatre in the heart of the West End, incorporating every convenience for the comfort of a new breed of theatre-goer.

• Seating capacity: 2,358.

ABOVE AND BELOW
A fatherly horned lion and a sphinx-like boy each play its part in Matcham's grand opus. Both details are to be found in the theatre's foyer.

he year was 1902, and the new-found opulence and bravado that came to typify Edwardian London were in full flow. King Edward VII exemplified the art of pleasure-seeking, particularly during the social 'Season', lasting from Easter to August, when both English and visiting American society had to be seen 'in Town'. For lesser mortals the corner pub provided solace among the endless rows of Victorian terraced houses filling out a rapidly expanding suburbia. In both city and suburbs there was 'new money' to be found, and elaborate variety theatres were more than ready to charm that money from willing pockets.

This was the background against which a new job came into the Holborn offices of Frank Matcham and Co.: the commission to interpret the ultimate vision of young entrepreneur Oswald (later Sir Oswald) Stoll, who in 1899 had created, with Edward Moss, 15 years his senior, the theatrical operator Moss Empires Ltd. What Stoll wanted was a grand new family-oriented variety theatre, the 'Theatre de Luxe' of London, to be built at the foot of St Martin's Lane, close to Trafalgar Square and the National Gallery. Matcham would certainly have been familiar with the area, having recently added the London Hippodrome (for Moss Empires), nearby in Charing Cross Road, to his tally of over 60 theatres designed and built during the previous 25 years. In the 18th century St Martin's Lane was best known for drinking and fighting, but by 1900 the rather jaded brick-fronted residential buildings on the theatre site, immediately north of the long, narrow Brydges Place (formerly Taylor's Buildings), were free from sin and ripe for redevelopment.

From the site the land falls steadily away to Trafalgar Square with its dominant Nelson's Column, fountains and pigeons, overlooked by the church of St Martin-in-the-Fields, James Gibbs's masterpiece of 1722; Matcham would have known that something very special was required of him among such illustrious neighbours. It would be of absolutely no use to create a building that

conformed to the rhythm and scale of the existing low-rise architecture; on the other hand, a gargantuan block would be equally inappropriate. Matcham solved the problem brilliantly, dividing the terracotta-faced (now painted) frontage by the deft use of a triple-arcaded ground storey, restricting its visual height to that of the existing adjacent buildings. His *pièce de résistance* was the introduction of an exuberant tower above the main entrance, at the southern end of the elevation, topped by a revolving illuminated globe bearing the word COLISEUM.

The free baroque asymmetrical façade is cleverly balanced by a pavilion tower at its northern end, in a relaxed yet controlled design from a man at the peak of his career. The linking body of the theatre is capped by a continuous balustrade behind which was a refreshment room within a glazed iron framework, a unique feature in a London theatre; it was removed in 1951. At the end of the 20th century all that remained of this elegant structure were graceful imprints on the tower walls. Entry is via a small, glazed semicircular canopy into an ornate vestibule with banded marble walls under an elaborate

Byzantine mosaic dome, signed Diesperser. Oddly, this Byzantine theme is quickly abandoned, and the spacious main foyer is comparatively delicate, relying for its welcoming qualities on cream and gold Adamesque ornament. The barrel-vaulted box office was originally a ladies' powder room.

Stoll's concept at the Coliseum was innovative in every sense, from the lifts provided for the convenience of the audiences to the royal lounge designed to move silently on tracks from the street to the royal box, where it would double as a retiring room. Presumably this did not work well, as it was almost immediately abandoned in favour of a small retiring room adjacent to the main foyer, redecorated for King George V (from which redecoration an amazing panelled WC and washbasin enclosure survives today), and a second, larger room behind the present royal box. Rising from the main foyer to the simple 'classical' dress-circle foyer is a superb grand staircase of stubby marble balusters and a heavy handrail. Long gone, however, are the tearooms at all levels, the baronial smoking hall and the state-of-the-art information bureau, a startlingly new idea in 1902.

The cream and pale blue auditorium, designed to seat over 3,000, is a wonderful three-tier space, richly ornamented in eclectic classical detail. Pairs of bow-fronted boxes under domed canopies adjoin niches originally designed to accommodate an auditorium choir, but now converted to boxes. Over the whole stretches a fine domed ceiling. Matcham was no stranger to modern engineering practices, and the cantilevered balconies make use of the finest early 20th-century technology.

Behind the 54-foot-wide proscenium arch, the Coliseum is quite massive in scale. It was originally fitted out with an innovative triple revolve incorporating an outer table 75 feet in diameter, all of which was removed in 1977. Seventy-one counterweight sets were provided, along with 10 sets of two-ton counterweights intended to raise particularly heavy props. In the 1970s a cyclorama track was in situ on the rear wall, but this was recently seen in pieces, lying on the stage of the disused Alexandra Palace Theatre in north London – whither it was almost certainly removed in a compromise effort to preserve it, there being in the late 1990s a sadly unfulfilled move to create a Museum of Theatre Technology.

Ellen Terry, Sarah Bernhardt and Diaghilev all appeared at the Coliseum in its early 20th-century glory days. Later, for seven years from 1961, it was used as a cinema before becoming home to the Sadler's Wells Opera Company, now the English National Opera. Long may it continue to be so.

ABOVE Everything about the Coliseum is on a large scale – the Grand Salon, the Grand Tier Tea Room, the Grand Staircase, the Baronial Smoking Room, even the Grand Entrance Hall – expressing a very clear message. That message is highlighted down to the smallest detail – here, in the use of a spectacular lion mask and suspended shield to carry two small lamps.

RIGHT Way above the auditorium a dusty charioteer controls what appears to be an team of angry lions with implausible ease.

LEFT High-quality metalwork, such as is found on this elevator gate, is quite rare in London's theatres, and illustrates the grand architectural vision of Frank Matcham and his client Sir Oswald Stoll.

LONDON PALLADIUM
ARGYLL STREET

HISTORY

- 1864. Argyll House, which previously occupied the site, is demolished.

- 1868. Corinthian Bazaar opens above commercial wine cellars.

- 1871. Hengler's Grand Cirque opens.

- 1895. Lease sold to National Skating Palace Ltd.

- 1908. Lease passes to Walter Gibbons.

- 1910. Palladium Theatre, designed by Frank Matcham, opens on Boxing Day.

- Statutorily Listed Historic Building: Grade II*.

OF SPECIAL INTEREST

- Classical temple-like façade to Argyll Street.

- The interior, a triumph of design and decoration.

- Seating capacity: 2,291.

ABOVE A lion mask terminates the immaculate polished handrail in the entrance vestibule.

RIGHT In the luxurious vestibule it is easy to appreciate how architect Frank Matcham managed to exceed his estimated building cost by some 25 per cent.

OPPOSITE The pedimented main façade to Argyll Street is crowned by a sculpted figure group representing Literature, Art and Science, with flanking figures supporting the comic and tragic masks of theatre.

ir Anthony Eden was Prime Minister, and Dwight D. Eisenhower was 34th President of the United States when, at 7pm on 25 September 1955, Independent Television broadcast the first *Sunday Night at the London Palladium* show, hosted by Tommy Trinder and staring Gracie Fields and Guy Mitchell. Post-war austerity lingered well into the 1950s, and the show's quality and lavish presentation (even in black and white) caught the public's imagination to a degree that ensured its continuation at intervals to the turn of the millennium. Here were stars who, until they appeared in those early broadcasts, had so often been heard only on gramophone records and seen only in publicity photographs and magazines. Compères succeeding Tommy Trinder, such as Bruce Forsyth, Norman Vaughan and Larry Grayson, were to become household names; and the weekly finale, as the cast took its curtain call on the stage revolve, made early television magic and ensured that the London Palladium would become probably the most famous variety theatre in the world.

ABOVE The almost unaltered interior is a tribute to the genius of Frank Matcham. The proscenium arch was temporarily remodelled to accommodate a production of *The King and I*.

Seeing the building on television, it would be difficult to imagine it as anything but a focal point in the heart of West End theatreland – but this is far from the case. The theatre is situated on the east side of Argyll Street, a short, narrow link-road between Oxford Street to the north and Great Marlborough Street to the south, running parallel with Regent Street. The area was undeveloped until 1670, when houses started to spring up either side of nearby Kingly Street, but it was not until the 1730s that Argyll Street and Little Argyll Street (opposite the theatre), named after John Campbell, 2nd Duke of Argyll, were laid out. Little remains of the original development apart from remnants of No. 8 Argyll Street, and continuous redevelopment has left the east side of the street with an irregular roofline in which a number of particularly tall buildings have reduced the visual impact of the theatre on the townscape. Close to the theatre two blue plaques, mounted by the Greater London Council, record

the residence at No. 8 of the American writer Washington Irving and, at No. 10, Major General William Roy, founder of the Ordnance Survey.

Of particular architectural merit in the street is Palladium House (formerly Ideal House, 1928), which occupies the eastern angle between Argyll Street and Great Marlborough Street. Designed by Gordon Jeeves and Raymond Hood as a miniature of Hood's National Radiator Corporation building in New York, it rises as a sheer black structure faced in Swedish granite, relieved only by the sparing use of cast bronze in yellow, gold, green and orange lotus and geometric patterns, mainly at a high level, resulting in an overall Egyptian feel.

On the site of the London Palladium stood Argyll House, home of the 2nd Duke until his death in 1743. The house remained in the family until 1808, when the 6th Duke sold it to the long-lived 4th Earl of Aberdeen. When he died in 1860, his family auctioned the house two years later, and it was sold

ABOVE The circle bar is lavishly decorated in a cream and gold French rococo style. The Long (upper circle) Bar, by contrast, is plain.

achieved by adding two galleries and a stage. After Hengler's death in 1887 the circus continued until 1895 when the National Skating Palace Ltd took over the building for four years.

In the early 1900s an attempt was made, with little success, to revive the circus, but in 1909 architect Frank Matcham was commissioned by lessee Walter Gibbons to design the Palladium, a variety theatre on a grand scale, at a final cost of some £250,000 (probably well in excess of £10 million in today's terms), exceeding the original estimate by some £50,000.

The cream-painted seven-bay pedimented frontage to the theatre, retained from the Corinthian Bazaar, has a classical temple-like quality. Three central bays form the main entrance at street level, with an open loggia above. To step up into the building from the undistinguished street into the white, gold and marble of the vestibule and staircase with their prolific 18th-century and rococo detailing, is in itself to experience a piece of true theatre. On the north side of the main entrance a corridor of nine cross-vaulted bays gives access to the advance-booking hall, which would amply accommodate a small bank.

The magnificent two-tier auditorium is a triumph of design, ornamented in a French rococo style: a tribute to the genius of Matcham as an architect of the first rank, notwithstanding the fact that the delightful white, gold and pink of the original colour scheme has now become a dreary chocolate brown with dull gold highlights, above a marble dado. Behind the proscenium arch, and under the stage, is the framework of the revolve, which contributed so much to the Sunday-night magic, complete with its mercury flask rectifiers, all dating from 1936. Sadly, it is proposed that it soon be removed to create much-needed additional space for the theatre.

In Great Marlborough Street, next to the former Marlborough Street Magistrates' Court, and on the site of the Argyll Baths, are the untidy but spacious stage-door approach and the dressing-room block.

On Boxing Day 1910 this great variety theatre opened, with tea being provided in the Palm Court at the rear of the stalls, accompanied by 'lady musicians in Pompadour gowns'. A great innovation was the installation of box-to-box telephones, early precursors to the mobile phone, plus the additional convenience of an in-house hairdresser's salon. This was the world of the Folies Bergères, the Crazy Gang, Barnum, *La Cage aux Folles*, *Joseph and His Amazing Technicolour Dreamcoat* and *The King and I*. The list of individual stars who have performed here is endless, but it includes Judy Garland, Duke Ellington, Sammy Davis Jnr, Ginger Rogers, Margot Fonteyn and many, many more.

again in 1863; the following year it was demolished and deeply excavated to accommodate a large commercial wine cellar owned by George Haig. Covering the cellar from 1868 was the Corinthian Bazaar, named after its columned façade on Argyll Street which now, although altered, still forms the principal façade to the theatre. The bazaar was a failure, and its successor, the Palais Royal Exhibition Rooms, was bought out around 1870 by F. C. Hengler. Hengler, an established circus owner and administrator, was being consulted on the conversion of the building to circus use, utilizing the Argyll Street frontage, with some rearrangement, as its entrance. In spite of its undisputed popularity Hengler's Grand Cirque, along with Nos. 6 and 7 Argyll Street, failed to meet a reserve of £65,000 when they were put up for auction in 1883 by G. A. Haig & Co. When Haig was unable to sell, Hengler took part of the lease and engaged architect C. J. Phipps to improve his circus building, which was

LYCEUM THEATRE
WELLINGTON STREET

ABOVE Rinceau
decoration
proliferates
in the Lyceum.

OPPOSITE In 1996
the ornate rococo
auditorium once
more played host
to thousands of
theatre-goers.

efore the extensive demolitions at the beginning of the 20th century that cleared the way for the creation of Aldwych and Kingsway, two theatres seemed to watch each other from either side of Wellington Street. To the west, almost over-looking the approach to Waterloo Bridge, was the Lyceum; to the east was the Gaiety, built in 1868 and closed for demolition on 4 July 1903. Wellington Street, running between Tavistock Street and the Strand, was only a little over 30 years old when the Gaiety was built, being an extension of Bow Street, and the then Charles Street, to the river. The Lyceum now looks at the rear of the former Morning Post building of 1907, designed by Mewès and Davis and faced in Norwegian granite.

The Lyceum began life as an exhibition and concert hall within the grounds of Exeter House, Strand, designed by James Paine for the Incorporated Society of Artists in 1765. Paine was a prolific architect, probably better known for his country houses, such as Wardour Castle, Wiltshire, and his extensive rebuilding at Alnwick Castle, Northumberland. He designed brilliantly in the Palladian manner, but faded from fashion as Robert Adam prospered with his reinterpretations of the style, introducing a wonderful array of previously unexplored details.

In 1794 the building was converted to theatre use by its owner, Dr Samuel Arnold, but he was unable to obtain a licence to present drama, and it was very soon let by the New Circus. Some time before 1799 it became the Lyceum Theatre, now in the ownership of Dr Arnold's son S. J. Arnold. Madame Tussaud held her first London Waxworks Exhibition in the building in 1802, and plays were put on, but without any great success. In 1809 the Theatre Royal, Drury Lane, was burnt down and the company decamped to the Lyceum during rebuilding works; this was good news for Samuel Arnold Jnr, in that he was able, following the company's departure in 1812, to retain his theatre licence. In 1815 he renamed the building the Theatre Royal English Opera House, and in 1816 had it rebuilt by architect Samuel Beazley to present mainly opera. However, in 1830 it was itself destroyed by fire, and Wellington Street was extended over the site. Beazley was commissioned to rebuild the theatre again, this time a little further to the west, and on 12 July 1834 it reopened as the Royal Lyceum and English Opera House. In 1856 it was taken over again, this time by the Covent Garden Theatre Company, whose building had burnt down.

The only architectural feature of Beazley's theatre extant today is the cream-painted stone Greco-Roman portico, but the building did survive intact until 1903, when extensive alterations demanded by the London County Council made it cheaper to demolish the major part of the structure in 1904.

The Lyceum will always be associated with two of the greatest names in 19th-century theatre, Sir Henry Irving and Ellen Terry. Born John Henry Brodribb in Somerset in 1838, Irving was educated in London. He learnt his art travelling with provincial companies mainly in the north of England, and returned to London and the Queen's Theatre, Long Acre, in 1867; here he met Ellen Terry. Pursuing his gift for playing theatre's less savoury characters, Irving first appeared at the Lyceum in January 1887, and became actor–manager in 1878.

RIGHT Architect Samuel Beazley's Greco-Roman portico of 1834 dominates the southern end of Wellington Street. A stone's throw to the north, at No. 26, Charles Dickens took offices and apartments.

site. The fortuitous declaration of war meant that the building remained standing, albeit in a virtually derelict state, until 1945, when instead of the anticipated demolition it was let to Mecca Ltd and reopened as a dance hall. It was from here that the popular television show *Come Dancing* was produced, and live entertainment continued until 1991 when the theatre closed. Between 1991 and 1996 a programme of restoration was undertaken by the Apollo Leisure Group, and on 31 October 1996 the long-dormant building was reopened by His Royal Highness the Prince of Wales.

The grand entrance foyer and staircase rise up in shades of red and light brown to Crewe's spectacular auditorium with its exuberant rococo decoration – its chunky cherubs and fruity swagging not enhanced, however, by the brown shades in which it is currently painted. Although much of the fabric is new, the theatre pays an undoubted tribute to the Apollo Leisure Group and to their architects, Halpern and Partners.

The first production staged here after the reopening was Andrew Lloyd Webber's *Jesus Christ Superstar*, and at the turn of the millennium it was Disney Productions' production of *The Lion King* that was filling the house.

ABOVE Detail of Bertie Crewe's exuberant rococo plasterwork decoration. A chubby cherub sits slightly uneasily on a palm seat.

He immediately engaged Ellen Terry to play Ophelia to his Hamlet, and that partnership was to survive until the summer of 1902, when they parted company. They had toured America eight times, and in 1895 Irving had become the first actor to be knighted. He died in 1905, but Ellen Terry continued her career, and was created dame in 1925; she died in 1928.

By December 1904 a new theatre, designed by Bertie Crewe, who had been chief assistant firstly to Walter Emden and then to W. G. R. Sprague, had been built and was opened to present melodrama to the public. Never hugely successful, it closed in July 1939, ostensibly for redevelopment, though the London County Council had its own plans for the

ABOVE Four pairs of elaborate timber entrance doors give access to the vestibule, with its broad hint of Art Nouveau.

LYRIC THEATRE
SHAFTESBURY AVENUE

ABOVE The
elliptical arched
proscenium is
highly decorated
with mythological
imagery.

RIGHT Part-
elevation of the
brick and stone
screen-wall front
to Shaftesbury
Avenue. This
architecture is
more simplistic
than in other
theatres of the
period, and may
well reflect the
theatre owner's
preoccupation
with profits.

wkwardly shaped sites in the West End were no hindrance to such entrepreneurs as Henry J. Leslie, who in 1886 took an 80-year lease from the Metropolitan Board of Works to build a theatre at the southern end of the newly opened Shaftesbury Avenue. He then purchased the freehold of the adjoining Café l'Etoile, which occupied the former house and museum of the 18th-century anatomist Dr William Hunter. The brick-faced building fronting onto Great Windmill Street was designed in 1767 by Scotsman Robert Mylne, a fine, prolific architect, to house Hunter's library, anatomical theatre and dissecting rooms as well as his living accommodation. Of the house, only the rather nondescript street elevation of painted brickwork survives, a London County Council blue plaque paying tribute to the great medical man.

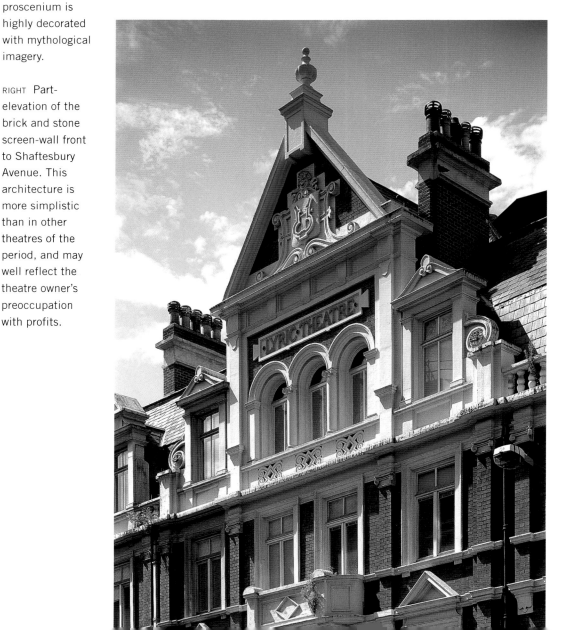

Leslie chose C. J. Phipps to design his theatre on what was, at the time, a virtually isolated site. He financed the development with the profits he made from Alfred Cellier and B. C. Stephenson's comic opera *Dorothy*, and saw it as a money-making concern. With the eye of an entrepreneur, Leslie stipulated that the building must incorporate rentable offices and chambers, a requirement that must have generated considerable discussion between architect and client.

Phipps planned his theatre, which opened in 1888, behind a 150-foot-long screen wall to Shaftesbury Avenue. Designed in an Italian–Flemish Renaissance manner, it is faced in red brick with stone dressings, bearing the name of the theatre carved in large letters above a central pavilion. The stage backs onto Great Windmill Street, with dressing rooms built into the remains of Hunter's house. Decorated in an Adamesque manner, the auditorium was originally pale lemon, white and gold,

with hangings of gold and coral brocatelle – appropriate colours which have been replaced by a less felicitous overall hue of warm, deepish salmon pink. At upper-circle level is the finest of the theatre's bars, presented as a 17th-century room but incorporating mid-18th-century detail. Included on the chimney piece are masks depicting the Green Man, a symbol of fertility, accompanied by what appears to be the Devil himself! Modifications to the entrance vestibule, crush room and stalls bar by Michael Osenauer in 1932, in a simple Odeon style, have done little to enhance the building.

An extensive list of successful productions extends from Wilson Barrett's *The Sign of the Cross* in 1896, through *The Chocolate Soldier*, a musical interpretation of Shaw's *Arms and the Man* (1910) and J. B. Priestley's *Dangerous Corner* (1932), to Alan Bennett's *Habeas Corpus* (1973), a success for the late Sir Alec Guinness and indeed Bennett himself, who appeared as Mrs Swabb.

NEW AMBASSADORS
THEATRE
WEST STREET

HISTORY

• 1912. Commissioned as one of a pair of new theatres to be designed by W. G. R. Sprague; opened on 5 June 1913.

• 1999. Renamed New Ambassadors Theatre to reflect a concentration on the country's best new works and most exciting companies and artists.

• Statutorily Listed Historic Building: Grade II.

OF SPECIAL INTEREST

• The masterly design which overcame a variety of site and planning restrictions.

• Seating capacity: 408.

ABOVE Fine ironmongery is evident in the door furniture.

RIGHT The façade cleverly turns the street corner above the main entrance. The elevation has deeply recessed windows and segmental pediments linked by the parapet design.

OPPOSITE PAGE Reflected in an attractive mirror, the Louis XVI-style auditorium suffers from being painted an overall cream. The basket-arched proscenium is flanked by a tall, semicircular headed box, while the curving dress-circle balcony sits slightly uncomfortably against the auditorium wall.

brief glance at erudite works on architecture such as James Stevens Curl's *Oxford Dictionary of Architecture* (1999) or Nikolaus Pevsner's *Buildings of England* series (various dates from 1951) is sufficient to show how rare it is to find more than passing reference to the great theatre architects, such as W. G. R. Sprague and C. J. Phipps – neither of whom rates space in the *Oxford Dictionary* – and the unsurpassed Frank Matcham – who is allotted a grudging eight lines. Sprague, subordinate to Matcham only in physical stature, was commissioned in 1912 to design the Ambassadors for Ambassadors Theatre Ltd, to be followed (three years later) by St Martin's Theatre, the two being separated by Tower Court (formerly Lumber Court), a pedestrian footway.

It is not readily apparent from the street, but the planning of the Ambassadors is the work of a master. The site is extremely restricted, to the north by the long established West Street Chapel, built around 1700 for French

LEFT A fine view of ribboned leaf decoration to the shallow-domed auditorium ceiling. Just below, within a semicircular arch, is a roundel holding an ambassadorial crest.

theatre, unhampered by any such height restriction, overshadows the earlier Ambassadors – but ironically the pair are now totally dominated by Orion House, a ponderous 14-storey block designed by Renton Howard Wood Levine Partnership (1990).

Small buildings and a corner pub were demolished to provide this vacant plot in an area where many artisan houses had been cleared to make way, in particular, for Sandringham Buildings, opposite the theatre. Opened by the Prince and Princess of Wales in 1884, these Gothic-style dwellings were designed to house some 1,500 poorer residents – a ready-made audience of working people earning an adequate amount of money and often quite happy to spend some of it at the playhouse.

The low-rise, three-storey stuccoed theatre, painted yellow and very pale blue, is entered on the angle, under a continuous canopy. The very restrained classical main elevation which curves into Tower Court is articulated by four central pilasters, flanked by more prominent channelled pilastered wings under segmental pediments. A single-bay wing repeats in Tower Court. The pretty foyer is of necessity small-scale; the deceptively grand Louis XVI-style auditorium, now painted cream apart from coloured ambassadorial crests at high level, was described in 1913 as being Parma violet, ivory and dull gold. The shallow curve of the dress circle, with its panelled front enhanced by bay-leaf swags and plain shields, has been placed unusually close to the proscenium. To the rear of the dress circle a second small circle is provided as a raised tier, and the shallow-domed auditorium ceiling is ornamented with heavily ribboned leaf decoration and central swags of fruit, flowers and musical instruments. Above the foyer is a small, cosy and quite attractive dress-circle bar. Of the timber stage machinery nothing survives.

The current management, which renamed the theatre the New Ambassadors in May 1999, intends to bring fresh new talent to London, embracing all aspects of the theatre. There are illustrious precedents: Vivien Leigh made her West End debut here in 1935; the Blitz failed to close the doors; and *The Mousetrap* was launched from here on 25 November 1952; so with good fortune the baton of success will be passed on to the new guardians of the fabric.

Protestant refugees and closely associated with John and Charles Wesley; to the south by Lumber Court; and upwards by a serious height limitation in respect of the law of Ancient Lights, namely the right of a building's owner to have daylight fall on his established windows – (a right struggled with some years later by Ewen Barr when he designed the Duchess Theatre in 1929). Thus it is that the later

NEW LONDON THEATRE

PARKER STREET

HISTORY

• 17th century. Site of an inn which became known as the Great Mogul.

• 1847. Renamed the Mogul Saloon.

• 1851. Became the Middlesex Music Hall.

• 1911. Rebuilt by Frank Matcham for Oswald Stoll and James Graydon and renamed New Middlesex Theatre of Varieties.

• 1919. Rehabilitated to reopen as the Winter Garden Theatre.

• 1959. Closed permanently and demolished 1965.

• 1971. Redevelopment begun with the New London Theatre forming part of a wider brief.

OF SPECIAL INTEREST

• The flexible auditorium, with great potential for audience–actor interaction.

• Seating capacity: 1,100.

ABOVE
Mannequins of the characters from *Cats*, the theatre's current long-running show, decorate the main profiled concrete circulation space.

RIGHT The sheer glazed façade to the New London Theatre was part of a wider overall design brief by Paul Tvrtkovic with Chew and Percival and Sean Kenny, 1971.

t the northern end of Drury Lane, before it enters High Holborn, large, modern office buildings tangle with 19th-century commercial blocks, while small houses and shops of the 18th and 19th centuries jostle with giants of the 1930s, such as the Freemasons' Hall in Great Queen Street, in a remarkably civilized manner. There has been an inn at No. 167 since at least the 17th century, when Sir Thomas Drury gave his name to what was already an ancient roadway. Nell Gwyn, one-time barmaid, orange seller and actress, had lodgings in the Lane and links with the inn, which by this time had become known as the Great Mogul. By the mid-19th century the area had generally deteriorated, but in 1847 No. 167 was rehabilitated, opening on 27 December as the Mogul Saloon. In 1851 it became the Middlesex Music Hall, probably in response to the opening of the

ABOVE An apparently
simple but superbly
interactive arena,
incorporating a 60-foot
diameter revolve. The
auditorium configuration
can be changed
electronically, as can the
seating rake. Although
seating an audience of
1,100, the auditorium
(seen here with the
settings for *Cats*) is
friendly without being
cramped. In 1971,
when it was built, this
theatre represented the
cutting edge of stage-
design technology.

St Martin's Music Hall (later the Queen's Theatre) in
Long Acre the previous year. Music hall in London
had its roots in the pubs of the 1830s and 1840s,
especially in the East End. Many pubs had song
rooms and concert rooms, often across the front of
the building at first-floor level, and these became
increasingly popular from the 1850s and 1860s.

The Middlesex, which occupied a relatively small
site halfway between Parker Street and Macklin
Street, was rebuilt in 1872 and again in 1891, but in
1911 the 'Old Mo' was demolished and rebuilt by
architect Frank Matcham for Oswald Stoll and
James Graydon, who had managed it since 1875 as
the New Middlesex Theatre of Varieties, in an externally rather lean, typically Edwardian red-brick and
stone style. In 1919 the building was sold and, after
being completely redecorated, was opened as the
Winter Garden Theatre. In 1959 it was closed after
a successful production of *Alice in Wonderland*,
having been sold on – ostensibly for redevelopment
– to Pearson Forsythe and Co., who immediately
encountered planning problems with the London
County Council. The now derelict building was sold
again to Charles Forte, and consent was obtained for
an all-embracing multi-use complex incorporating

shops, restaurants, car parking, flats – and a theatre.
Matcham's theatre was demolished in 1965, but the
implementation of the scheme for which consent
had been granted, designed by architect Paul
Tvrtkovic with Chew and Percival and Sean Kenny
for Star Holdings Ltd, was not started until 1971.

The development as a whole contrasts with
rather than respects the scale and character of its
close neighbours. The theatre – sited on the southwest angle of the plot – while appearing to have its
roots firmly in the Royal Festival Hall, is not
enhanced by the sheer-profiled metal box that rises
above the impressive glazed front. Internally, the
profiled, shuttered concrete fails to lift the spirits in
an entrance vestibule overpowered by the raking
underside of a main access stairway as it rises to the
first-level foyer and bar.

The simple, largely black auditorium has been
carefully designed, literally 'in the round', to be
extremely flexible, incorporating the 60-foot revolve
and seats and walls whose positions are adjusted
electronically. The architect's imaginative approach
to his brief has produced a superb interactive arena
for actors and audience, with almost every detail
having received positive in-depth consideration.

OLD VIC THEATRE
WATERLOO ROAD

HISTORY

• 1818. Theatre designed by Rudolph Cabanel of Aachen.

• 1871. Reconstruction by architect J. T. Robinson.

• 1920s. Alterations by architect F. G. M. Chancellor.

• 1983. Extensive works by Renton Howard Wood Levine for owner Edwin Mirvish.

• Statutorily Listed Historic Building: Grade II*.

OF SPECIAL INTEREST

• As an architectural entity of early date, its importance is difficult to overestimate.

• Seating capacity: 1,066.

ABOVE A coat-of-arms-like detail fronted by a lyre adorns the upper-circle balcony front.

RIGHT Front elevation to The Cut. The theatre has been restored by architects Renton Howard Wood Levine, the works including the auditorium and the remodelling of front-of-house circulation spaces.

aterloo Road cannot be said to ooze charm as it leaves the southern end of Waterloo Bridge to pass Waterloo Railway Station. However, in this architectural desert a single building stands apart: the Old Vic, prominently sited on the southeast angle of Waterloo Road and The Cut, some 800 yards from the bridge. Once hemmed in by terraced housing, the theatre stands in a setting that has been radically altered by war damage and redevelopments since the late 1920s. To the west is a large open green space where once stood St Thomas's School, and to the rear are the impressive offices designed in 1930 by Payne Wyatt for David Greig, who opened his first grocery store in 1876 and went on to establish a successful chain.

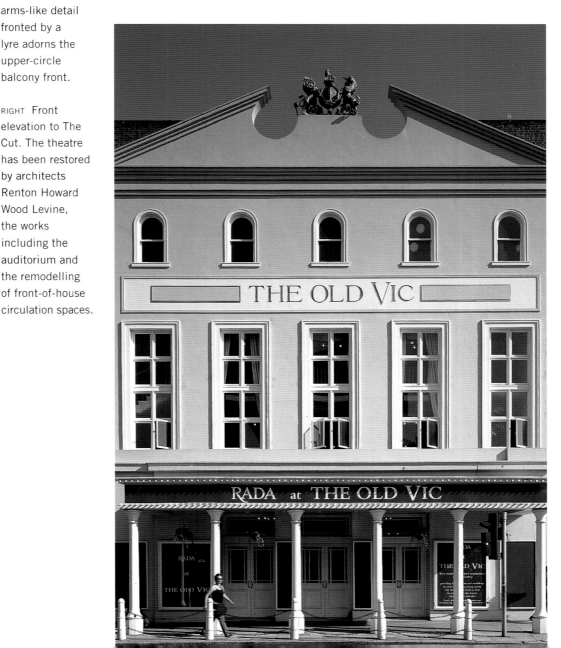

ABOVE Three tiers of very pretty paired boxes, restored to their original 19th-century glory by renowned theatre architects Renton Howard Wood Levine, flank the proscenium.

stone by proxy on 14 September 1816 on behalf of His Serene Highness the Prince of Saxe-Coburg and Princess Charlotte of Wales (though the royal couple had to be tactfully cajoled into becoming associated with the theatre). Charlotte, the daughter of King George IV and Queen Caroline, had married Prince Leopold on 2 May the same year; the marriage was to end all too soon when Charlotte died in childbirth on 5 November 1817.

The auditorium was decorated in a restrained fawn and gold, with the drop curtain bearing a view of Claremont House in Surrey, the home of the Prince and Princess. Although the press described the opening-night audience as 'large and fashionable', the theatre was designed for melodrama and pantomime, entertaining audiences of 'very doubtful reputation'. The present-day front, designed by Renton Howard Wood Levine, is loosely based on the 1818 original, with its broken pediment above five semicircular headed windows, and larger sash windows to the first floor. The canopied entrance replaces five doorways within recessed arches.

As a well-anticipated gesture of approval to the Queen-in-waiting, the theatre was renamed the Royal Victoria Theatre in July 1833. In 1871 the auditorium was remodelled by J. T. Robinson, an architect of considerable sensitivity and Frank Matcham's father-in-law, after which the theatre reopened as the New Victoria Theatre. Sold in 1874, it reopened once more in the same year as the Royal Victoria Palace Theatre. In 1880 it was altered again, and this time when it reopened it was as a temperance music hall, the brainchild of social reformer Emma Cons, an associate of John Ruskin and Octavia Hill. Cons' reformist purposes were clearly signalled in a changed name: first the Royal Victoria Coffee Tavern and then the Royal Victoria Coffee Music Hall. In 1898 she persuaded her niece, Lilian Baylis, to return from her adopted home in Johannesburg to become assistant manager, a post she held until Emma Cons' death in 1914, after which she took over in her own right. By her own admission not well educated, Lilian Baylis was religious but, at the same time, broad-minded, and she quickly jettisoned temperance to create the People's Opera House as the home of Shakespeare. She also acquired the Sadler's Wells Theatre, which opened in 1931 as 'the North London Old Vic', and alternated ballet and opera between the two houses until her death in 1937. While Emma Cons is remembered through a conservative bronze wall tablet in the theatre, Lilian Baylis, fittingly, gives her name to the upper-circle bar.

The completion of Sir John Rennie's Waterloo Bridge in 1817 ensured the viability of a theatre removed from the established artistic confines of the north riverbank. There have been seven name changes since it was opened in 1818 and a considerable number of both major and minor alterations, but without any doubt the Old Vic is of outstanding importance, both architecturally and as one of England's oldest theatres.

Designed by Rudolph Cabanel of Aachen, the long, yellow stock-brick flank walls defined by 11 bays of blind arcading are original and built up on stone from the demolished Savoy Hospital. Internally, the original system of heavy timber roof trusses survives hidden from view. A discreet foundation stone let into the west wall of the building records its origins as the First Royal Coburg Theatre. Alderman Goodbehere laid the

ABOVE Essentially architect J. T. Robinson's auditorium of 1871, and one of England's oldest surviving theatres. Lyre-plan balconies are supported on iron columns, and heavily moulded convex fronts and restored boxes complete an ensemble of the greatest moment.

During the 1920s the late Frank Matcham's chief assistant, the uninspired F. G. M. Chancellor, who was to rebuild Sadler's Wells in 1931, made extensive alterations, including the refronting of the building. In 1941 the theatre was damaged by enemy bombing and for nine years it remained closed, reopening in 1950; In 1963 the Old Vic was 'refurbished' again when it became the temporary home of the National Theatre under Sir Laurence Olivier. The Canadian Edwin Mirvish bought the Old Vic in 1982, commissioning architects Renton Howard Wood Levine to remodel the front of house; they created lightweight, modestly decorated, user-friendly spaces, contrasting well with the superb quality of Robinson's gold, cream and grey auditorium with its horseshoe balconies supported on iron columns.

Although the proscenium arch has been tam-pered with by, among others, Wells Coates in 1930, Sean Kenny in 1963, and again by Renton Howard Wood Levine in 1983 the restoration of the 1871 auditorium has been exemplary, includ-ing the conservation of Robinson's ceiling. Sadly, building archaeology rarely extends in depth to theatres, which – like pubs – seem to attract com-paratively little attention and support. Records have, of course, been made and papers written; but theatre structures such as the Old Vic have so much to say to the philologist who has learnt to interpret their language.

In recent years the spectrum of plays staged here has been wide, from *The Corn Is Green*, starring Deborah Kerr (1985), and *Ross* with Simon Ward (1986), to *Pride and Prejudice* (also 1986), *The Wars of the Roses* (1989) and *A Christmas Carol* with Patrick Stewart (1994).

PALACE THEATRE
CAMBRIDGE CIRCUS

ABOVE This
attractive trailing
plaster decoration
is among the
many surviving
gems at the
Palace Theatre.

OPPOSITE Sir
John Betjeman
believed the
Palace Theatre
to be 'London's
noblest surviving
building'.
Designed by one
of England's
finest architects,
T. E. Collcutt,
it occupies an
island site
overlooking
Cambridge
Circus, and
although it
has lost a
considerable
amount of
terracotta
ornament, there
cannot be any
doubt that it
remains a superb
work of art.

e shall never be privy to the thoughts of the Duke of Cambridge when he opened Charing Cross Road to the public for the first time in February 1887, but as he surveyed the poor quality of the new architecture he must have wondered at the almost unprecedented opportunities lost both here and in Shaftesbury Avenue. Cambridge Circus, named after the Duke, was an attempt to create a unified whole, but carried out with little sense of the dramatic and with minimal design impact, mainly in red brick and dressed stone. It is to the buildings of the 18th and early 19th centuries in surrounding streets, such as Romilly Street and Greek Street, that one has to look for a superior quality in scale and design.

While the blocks of offices, chambers and shops were filling the sites along the new roads, Richard D'Oyly Carte was discussing with the Metropolitan Board of Works the acquisition of the prime irregular quadrilateral island site on the west side of Cambridge Circus. Negotiations reached a conclusion, and on 15 December 1888 his second wife, Helen, laid the foundation stone of his new opera house.

D'Oyly Carte was born locally, in Greek Street, on 3 May 1844. After studying at University College, London, he worked with his father as a maker of musical instruments for the army, until setting up as a concert agent in 1870. Eminently successful, he 'discovered' Gilbert and Sullivan, probably through their production of *Thespis* in 1871, and in 1875 produced their *Trial By Jury* at the Royalty Theatre. Success followed upon success, and profits soared to such heights that D'Oyly Carte was able to finance the building of the Savoy Theatre in 1881. An opera-loving speculator, he resolved to build a London theatre devoted to grand English opera, and the vacant plot on Cambridge Circus appeared to be the ideal site.

Architect J. G. Buckle was commissioned to advise on the original design concept, and his adventurous steel-framed cantilevering of the royal tier stalls, the first circle and the amphitheatre provided an inspired skeletal form around which to build. Unusually, D'Oyly Carte dispensed with a contractor and took upon himself the supervision of building works alongside G. H. Holloway, whose buildings already included the Savoy Hotel and the Hotel Metropole. It was not until the ground works were well advanced that another architect, T. E. Collcutt, was engaged to give architectural substance to the interior and exterior of the building.

Thomas Collcutt was born in Oxford in 1840 and educated at Mill Hill School. He was articled in London, and lived most of his life at Totteridge, Middlesex, in the beautiful Arts and Crafts-style house he designed overlooking the green. A Gothicist at heart, Collcutt was forced to adapt to fluctuating taste, thus developing a hybrid Tudor–Renaissance style and winning, in 1886, the competition for the Imperial Institute in South Kensington. Not a specialist in theatre design, Collcutt saw the D'Oyly Carte commission purely as a piece of architecture, much as he would a small country house, or commercial building: a project to be given the profound consideration of an academic mind.

The exterior of the building is designed in a northern French Renaissance manner, in red brick and terracotta. The bricks are a dark red from the Ellistown Brickworks, an offshoot of the Leicestershire coal-mining industry, and the

delicately figured buff terracotta work was provided by the Lambeth firm of Doulton and Co. The slightly concave front to the building echoes the curve of the Circus, articulated by octagonal corbelled domed corner towers and turrets. After a century of attack from a fume- and grime-laden atmosphere, the terracotta has lately required fairly extensive repair and replacement. Initial attempts to clean the building in the latter decades of the 20th century regrettably resulted in some surface erosion caused by over-enthusiastic sandblasting.

Although the theatre opened as the Royal English Opera House on 31 January 1891, numerous variations in the design continued to be made up to 1893. However, notwithstanding these minor hiccups, the interior is quite sumptuous: Algerian and Italian marbles were lavishly used not only on the grand staircase, but also in vestibules, saloons and even the auditorium. Painted wall decoration in green and gold, arabesques and allegorical figures served only to emphasize the accomplishment of the design. As a

ABOVE Advanced construction and grand design come together at the Palace. Three tiers of boxes flank a lavishly decorated proscenium arch, faced in marbles and onyx, while the tympanum above the proscenium is ornamented with allegorical figures.

final touch, the carpets throughout were designed by William Morris.

The care that D'Oyly Carte devoted to the public parts of the theatre extended also behind the proscenium arch, where he not only introduced a revolutionary flat stage, but also employed engineer Walter Dando to put in a wood-and-iron set of stage machinery. This machinery was to be based on a French model of chariot and pole, designed to combine stability with the efficient and smooth movement of set-piece and ground-row scenery. Having lain disused for many years, the timbering is now reduced to a substantial archaeological relic, and is likely to be removed within the next few years. Although enough remains for a restoration

programme to be carried out (in an ideal world), the theatre on its confined island site is desperately in need of additional space, and that space, by definition, must be found under the stage.

D'Oyly Carte opened with Sir Arthur Sullivan's *Ivanhoe* (1891) and followed up with Messager's *The Basoche* (1892). The fact that he was unable to stage an English opera as his second presentation depressed him, and after a season starring Sarah Bernhardt in a series of French dramas, including plays by Sardou, Moreau, Dumas and Racine, he sold the building to Augustus Harris, who renamed it the Palace Theatre of Varieties in 1892. D'Oyly Carte's health deteriorated, and on 3 April 1901 he died at Hastings, Sussex.

Since then, many great names have passed through the stage door, including Marie Tempest in 1906; Maud Allen as Salome in 1908; and the inimitable Pavlova in 1911, followed by Nijinsky in 1914. In 1921 Harry Lauder appeared for eight weeks in a variety bill, and in 1933 Fred Astaire starred in *Gay Divorcee*. As the decades passed, in 1959 short seasons included vehicles for Johnnie Ray and Connie Francis, and in 1961 *The Sound of Music* opened here, followed by *Cabaret* (1968), *Oklahoma!* (1980) and, on 4 December 1985, *Les Misérables*.

In a sad footnote it must be said that while much has been achieved in the repair and cleaning of the exterior of this remarkable building, the interior is desperately in need of a (vastly expensive) cleaning and restoration programme which would restore life to D'Oyly Carte's vision, and one of Europe's premier theatres.

'The world's greatest artistes have passed and will pass through these doors'
Inscribed in the lintel above the stage door

LEFT The grand staircase, richly faced in Italian and Algerian marbles, rises from the south side of the main entrance foyer, planned on three sides of an open wall, the whole handled with the panache of a master designer.

ABOVE The mirrored walls along the staircase that leads to the stalls show off the theatre's ornate plasterwork to excellent effect.

PHOENIX THEATRE
CHARING CROSS ROAD

HISTORY

• 1930. Designed for Sidney Lewis Bernstein by Bertie Crewe, Cecil Masey, Theodore Komissarjevsky and Sir Giles Gilbert Scott.

• Statutorily Listed Historic Building: Grade II.

OF SPECIAL INTEREST

• Interior by Theodore Komissarjevsky, his first theatre design.

• Painted panels and safety curtain by Vladimir Polunin.

• Collection of cartoons housed in stalls bar.

• Seating capacity: 1,020.

ABOVE High-quality pilaster ornament within the auditorium.

RIGHT
Vladimir Polunin's painted panels and safety curtain are dominant elements of the Italian Renaissance interior.

ome hundred yards north of Cambridge Circus, and on the line of the west boundary wall to the former medieval Hospital of St Giles, the stuccoed entrance to the Phoenix Theatre blends with its conjoined neighbour, an unprepossessing six-storey block of offices above shops, as it curves into the narrow confines of Flitcroft Street, where the Elms Lester scene-painting workshop of 1903–4 is a rare survival of its kind. Opposite the entrance in Charing Cross Road is the Central St Martin's College of Art and Design (1939) and an interesting former pub, the Tam O'Shanter (1876), while between the two is the remnant of what appears to be a small early cinema.

Like so many others, the theatre was built on land formerly occupied by run-down properties; in this case including a corner pub, but in particular the Alcazar, a 'music hall' of rather dubious moral character. That name is now perpetuated in a block of flats close by in Phoenix Street, which forms the southern boundary to the theatre. Also in Phoenix Street is the present main theatre entrance, whose classical style contrasts markedly with the Art Deco of the Charing Cross façade. Formerly linked to the now demolished Curzon Cinema, the front is dominated by its wide central Portland-stone bay, which features twisted Ionic columns under a richly decorated entablature and modillion cornice above three pairs of enriched doors. To either side are single-window wide brick bays.

In the late 1920s Sidney Lewis Bernstein, later Lord Bernstein, assembled a unique quartet of architect–designers to create his theatre on lands owned by the

RIGHT Three pairs of enriched timber doors under decorative fanlights give access from the narrow confines of Phoenix Street. Triple-arched window openings extend through the first and second floors between Ionic twisted columns; the metal window frames are typical of the 1930s.

cinemas for Bernstein through the following decade, including the masterpiece of the Granada Cinema, Tooting, and such minor classics as the Granada, Harrow Weald, Middlesex (both 1937). Komissarjevsky was born in Venice of Russian parents and trained in architecture. He came to England in 1919 aged 27, making an indelible impression on English theatre with quite exceptional productions in his converted cinema at Barnes in West London. The fourth member of the team, Sir Giles Gilbert Scott, is harder to place in this company; since 1903 he had been deeply involved with the building of the great Anglican Cathedral in Liverpool, with Ampleforth Abbey and College, Yorkshire also on his drawing board. In 1947, aged 67, he would begin work on Bankside Power Station, now the Tate Modern Gallery, close to Shakespeare's Globe.

Contrasting entrances lead through to contrasting foyers. Behind the Charing Cross Road frontage is a very pretty circular domed enclosure decorated in shades of blue and cream, accessed by two pairs of enriched doors glazed with 14 bevelled lights. Entering from Phoenix Street, one sees richly coloured coffering and grotesque scrollwork dominating a marble staircase adorned with decorative detail in an 18th-century style. Rich decoration extends throughout the building. For his first theatre design Komissarjevsky chose a loose but masterly Italian Renaissance style, with nine painted panels in the auditorium and a superb painted safety curtain by Vladimir Polunin. The attractive circular inner stalls vestibule is enhanced by an elaborate mirrored ceiling, and a visit to the plushy Phoenix Stalls Bar will be rewarded by a small but exceptional collection of cartoons from the likes of Bill Tidy, David Langdon and Quentin Blake, lampooning the Phoenix.

The blue, pink and gold colour scheme of the opening night is perpetuated in spirit, enlivened by recent in-house decoration repeating exactly the previous colour scheme – thus sidestepping the need to make application to the local council and to English Heritage for listed building consent, which would probably be required on the grounds that any deviation from the existing colours could be interpreted as changing the character of the building.

Since its opening production of Noël Coward's comedy *Private Lives* on 24 September 1930, the theatre has seen many successes, ranging from *Late Night Final* (1931) through *Family Affairs* with Margaret Lockwood (1935) to *Dancing at Lughnasa* starring Alec McCowen (1991).

ABOVE The flat coffered ceiling and grotesque scrollwork lend an air of Renaissance opulence to the entrance foyer from Phoenix Street.

Brinkman Estate. Bertie Crewe, who had designed the Metropole, Birmingham, as early as 1885, was joined by Cecil Masey, whose Empire in Edmonton, north London, was under construction in 1908. While Crewe was nearing the end of his working life in 1930, Masey would collaborate with Theodore Komissarjevsky to produce super-

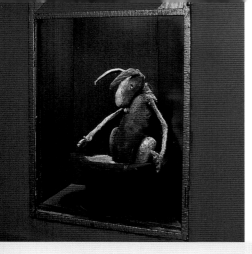

PICCADILLY THEATRE
DENMAN STREET

HISTORY

• 1928. Theatre built on site of derelict stables and a pub to the designs of Bertie Crewe and Edward A. Stone, for the Piccadilly Theatre Company.

OF SPECIAL INTEREST

• Mural panels in the Ladies' Bar by Stuart Robertson and Phillip O'Reilly, painted in 1988.

• Seating capacity: 1,200.

ABOVE A plump 'cricket' presides, mysteriously, at the Piccadilly.

way from the noise and urgency of Piccadilly Circus, the streets to its north, developed in the later 17th century, take on an air of anonymity; Glasshouse Street and Sherwood Street are little more than short cuts – particularly for taxis – from Regent Street to Soho, while small restaurants occupy Denman Street. Close by is the entrance to Piccadilly Circus underground station, and on the oblique angle between Glasshouse Street and Sherwood Street is the main entrance to the Regent Palace Hotel, immortalized by Sir John Betjeman in his poem 'The Flight From Bootle'. A grand faience-faced structure, designed in 1912 by Sir Henry Tanner (who also designed the Dickins and Jones store opposite the London Palladium), it dominates the Piccadilly Theatre.

The theatre's corner site, between Sherwood Street and Denman Street, was bought (probably very cheaply) by the Piccadilly Theatre Company in the late 1920s as a range of derelict stables and a pub, showing clearly on the 1875 edition Ordnance Survey map. The architects for the new building were Bertie Crewe, who was already working on the Phoenix Theatre, and Edward A. Stone, who also designed the Whitehall Theatre (1930). As an architect, Stone was safe rather than adventurous; his practice, later the respected Stone, Toms and Partners, built not only theatres but also atmospheric cinemas for Paramount, as well as the Warner Leicester Square (1938) – ironically on the site of Daly's Theatre, designed in 1893 by Spencer Chadwick and C. J. Phipps.

Externally the building cannot be said to be dramatic. Rising to three main storeys, plus attics above a modillion cornice, the stucco elevation drops down Sherwood Street, punctuated by standard metal windows, in 12 bays, divided at first- and second-floor levels by fat, giant pilasters. The front curves gently into Denman Street to stop rather abruptly on a projecting pavilion, which has

RIGHT Anthemion decoration ornaments the Piccadilly's original door furniture with style and confidence.

While scarcely qualifying as dramatic, the curving stuccoed façade descends with some dignity into Denman Street.

RIGHT The gaily decorated safety curtain enlivens an otherwise plain auditorium that dates from 1928.

absorbed the original pub in reduced form. A full-length canopy extends above a channelled and arcaded ground storey.

Internally, the small semicircular foyer retains an attractive Art Deco ticket office, and the auditorium approaches are enlivened by Vitruvian scroll friezes, a feature borrowed from the elevational treatment of the Regent Hotel. Marc Henri, working around the same time on the Duchess Theatre, produced a green and gold interior decoration scheme which fell victim to reconstruction works in the early 1960s. Eros is depicted to some effect on original etched glass display cabinets in the main staircase angles. The pink and gold, generally wallpapered auditorium, with its shallow serpentine balcony and

box fronts and plain ceiling, is unexciting. The bars, too, are plain, but the small Ladies' Bar which opens off the stalls has three mural panels of some interest painted by Stuart Robertson and Phillip O'Reilly in September 1988. Good original timber doors are retained throughout the building.

The theatre opened on 27 April 1928 with a production of *Blue Eyes* by Jerome Kern starring Evelyn Laye, but that same year it became a cinema showing early talkies such as *The Singing Fool* with Al Jolson. While not without successes, such as *Oliver!* in 1967 and *Gypsy* starring Angela Lansbury in 1973, the theatre is, maybe by virtue of its site, visually reclusive, and perhaps unfairly neglected by theatre-goers.

PLAYHOUSE THEATRE
CRAVEN STREET

ABOVE Bucranium ornament forms part of a triglyphed, swagged frieze under the dress circle.

HISTORY

• 1882. The Royal Avenue Theatre opens, designed by F. H. Fowler for Sefton Parry.

• 1905. Cyril Maude initiates comprehensive rebuilding programme, but partial collapse of Charing Cross Station on 5 December temporarily halts work.

• 1906. Architects Blow and Billerey commissioned to remodel interior of building.

• 1907. Theatre reopens on 28 January as The Playhouse.

• Statutorily Listed Historic Building: Grade II.

OF SPECIAL INTEREST

• Interior of unusually high quality.

• Timber stage machinery from the 1882 build.

• Seating capacity: 786.

RIGHT The line of the balustered upper boxes flows a little uncomfortably from the circle front, supported by golden caryatids and elaborate brackets flanking the stalls boxes either side of the deep proscenium.

n the Thames Embankment, close to Embankment Underground Station, the Playhouse Theatre is removed from London's theatrical epicentre. It occupies a site at the foot of Craven Street, a short distance from No. 36 where, between 1757 and 1762, the American scientist and statesman Benjamin Franklin lived. The theatre appears somehow trapped between the sheer face of the railway bridge as it enters Charing Cross Station and the overscaled buildings of Whitehall Court. Opposite the theatre is an attractive and quite rare surviving example of a green-painted and timber-boarded cabmen's shelter. Close by is London's single public memorial to W. S. Gilbert: a modest bronze plaque by Sir George Frampton – sculptor of Peter Pan in Kensington Gardens and Nurse Edith Cavell outside the National Portrait Gallery – inconspicuously fixed to the Embankment wall.

The first playhouse on this site, the Royal Avenue Theatre, was designed by F. H. Fowler and built in 1882 as a daring enterprise by the speculator Sefton Parry, gambling that when the South Eastern Railway Company needed to widen the station access, it would pay an extortionate sum of money for the building. Regrettably for Parry, this never happened. Originally of two storeys and faced in Portland stone, the restrained French Renaissance façade of eleven

architect Graham Berry, it has altered the relationship of scale between the buildings, and as if to exacerbate the situation the group is now dominated dramatically by Terry Farrell's much praised rebuilding of Charing Cross Station (1987–90).

In 1905 Cyril Maude became theatre manager, and immediately set about remodelling the building, again commissioning Fowler. The work progressed well until 5 December, when disaster struck: part of the railway station collapsed onto the

ABOVE Away from the auditorium a rather more restrained approach is apparent.

ABOVE RIGHT Although designed with great care by architect Graham Berry, the additional attic storey to F. W. Fowler's façade has altered its scale quite dramatically.

bays curves gracefully to abut the railway bridge. At the time of its construction the scale of the building, crowned by an open balustrade and sculpted figures, sat comfortably with the adjacent mid-18th-century brick terraced houses; but much has changed since then. For 10 years prior to 1987 the future of the theatre had looked bleak, until Robin Gonshaw, a loyal friend and supporter of the Playhouse, bravely undertook a comprehensive restoration programme, financed in part by the creation of offices, known as Aria House, in a third attic storey above the building. Although the expansion was carefully planned in detail by

theatre, killing six workmen and injuring many more. Handsome compensation was paid by the railway company and rebuilding began again, within the existing outer envelope, this time to the more fashionable designs of Blow and Billerey; most of the design work was executed by the Beaux Arts architect Ferdinand Billerey, in a Louis XV style. Perhaps hoping to change his luck, Maude renamed the theatre the Playhouse.

The quietly elegant cream and gold foyer and plain main staircase herald an auditorium representing a sumptuous exercise in splendour. The basket-arch proscenium, crowned by Thalia, one of

ABOVE This view, taken at dress-circle level, shows an auditorium quite exciting in appearance while ignoring the strict rules of architecture. The dark oval-panelled ceiling and the basket-arched wall panels seem somehow out of place in an otherwise bright interior.

the three daughters of Zeus and 'a delight to the gods and men', is flanked by boxes supported on caryatids. Serpentine balconies have turned baluster fronts, the upper level sitting uncomfortably against painted wall-panel decoration. Under the dress circle is a bold triglyph and bucranium frieze.

Under the stage the timber machinery, which almost certainly dates from 1882, is well preserved, and second in quality only to that surviving in Her Majesty's Theatre. Splendidly rerigged and repaired by David Wilmore of Theatresearch in 1987, it comprises a grave-trap, one corner trap, three bridges and a thunder run. Iron crab winches remain in situ on

the mezzanine, as do a number of trip levers. Above the stage, to accommodate Aria House, the original grid has been lowered, losing, in the process, four fine timber drums used to fly heavy scenery or props; the compromising of this superb late-19th-century stage must be regarded as extremely regrettable.

In 1950 the British Broadcasting Corporation took over the theatre, and it was from here that comedy classics such as *The Goon Show* and *Hancock's Half Hour* were recorded. Recent stage successes have included *The Rose Tattoo* starring Julie Walters and *Tartuffe* with Felicity Kendal (both 1991–2).

PRINCE EDWARD
THEATRE

OLD COMPTON STREET

HISTORY

- 1930. Designed by Edward A. Stone with Marc Henri and Gaston Laverdet.

- 1936. Converted to cabaret–restaurant use.

- 1939. Becomes services boxing club.

- 1946. Restored by T. and P. Braddock for theatrical performances.

- 1954. Converted to Cinerama.

- 1978. Returned to theatrical use.

- 1993. Rehabilitation programme by architects Renton Howard Wood Levine for Bernard Delfont and Cameron Mackintosh.

OF SPECIAL INTEREST

- The high-quality restoration of a theatre which had, over a protracted period, suffered many detrimental changes.

- Seating capacity: 1,619.

ABOVE The elegance of this typically Art Deco figure contrasts strongly with the heavier quality of the theatre's architecture.

RIGHT Simple Art Deco occupies a quiet corner of this theatre, built to provide a home for large-scale musicals.

ince its beginnings at the end of the 17th century, Old Compton Street – named after Henry Compton, former vicar of the now ruined St Anne's Church, Soho, Dean of the Chapel Royal and Bishop of London – has evolved as a busy, sometimes quite exotic, range of small shops and bars, with, particularly in its early days, a decidedly French flavour. A matter of yards away at 49 Dean Street, almost opposite St Anne's Church, is the French House, a pub frequented by actors, artists and poets, including Dylan Thomas and Brendan Behan, that became the headquarters of the Free French Forces during the Second World War.

If one looks about one from a position in front of the theatre, which occupies the angle with Greek Street, it would seem perfectly feasible to drown in an ocean of pleasure without going very far at all, surrounded as one is by restaurants of infinite variety, strip bars, sex shops, 'models at first floor, please ring', cinemas and theatres. Built on the site of a draper's shop known as The Emporium, the Prince Edward uncomfortably resembles a cinema. It was competently if slightly forbiddingly designed in 1930 by Edward A. Stone, architect of the Whitehall and Piccadilly Theatres, with interior works in fuchsia and gold by French designers Marc Henri and Gaston Laverdet, who also worked at the Whitehall and Piccadilly. The English palazzo-style building sits heavily: raised above a polished granite base, the building is faced in finely laid brown brick with deeply recessed joints, the front elevation relieved to some extent by its stuccoed attic storey and green shuttered windows under heavily bracketed and coffered eaves. At ground level a modern canopy, added in 1993, shelters five pairs of brass entrance doors.

Inside, a large, welcoming circular foyer gives access to the surprisingly grand auditorium, revitalized in 1993 by architects Renton Howard Wood Levine, through the inspirational drive of Bernard (later Lord) Delfont and Cameron Mackintosh. The whole is decorated in a combination of deep red and old gold. Prior to 1993, the theatre had undergone a catalogue of changes. Opening on 3 April 1930, it was converted in 1936 to a cabaret–restaurant and renamed the London Casino. Opening on 2 April that same year, the theatre closed again in 1939 to become a services boxing club. At the end of the war, theatre use was restored until 1954, when the relatively short-lived Cinerama craze came to London. The year 1978 saw live shows and almost immediate success restored to the theatre, with Elaine Paige starring in both *Evita* (1978) and *Chess* (1986), followed in 1989 by Cole Porter's *Anything Goes* and *Mama Mia* in 1999.

RIGHT A view that reveals the full splendour of the auditorium, restored in 1993 by architects Renton Howard Wood Levine.

PRINCE OF WALES
THEATRE
COVENTRY STREET

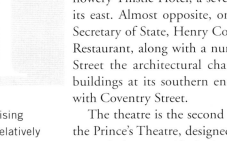

HISTORY

• 1884. Prince's Theatre designed by C. J. Phipps for actor–manager Edgar Bruce.

• 1886. Theatre renamed Prince of Wales.

• 1937. Old theatre demolished; in June, foundation stone of new theatre laid by Gracie Fields; in October, replacement theatre, designed by Robert Cromie, opens.

• Statutorily Listed Historic Building: Grade II.

OF SPECIAL INTEREST

• Superb collection of framed and dated playbills, assembled by theatre manager Mike Churchill, exhibited in the stalls bar.

• Seating capacity: 1,130.

ABOVE Rising from a relatively plain main foyer, the decorated stair well is a distinct bonus.

RIGHT
A remarkable survival in the stalls bar is the glass block bar counter, originally back-lit. The area behind the bar is enhanced with a lovingly assembled collection of playbills.

he Prince of Wales is situated on the eastern angle of Oxenden Street, about halfway between Piccadilly Circus and Leicester Square, adjacent to the more flowery Thistle Hotel, a seven-storey, late-19th-century Portland-stone block to its east. Almost opposite, on Coventry Street – named after King Charles II's Secretary of State, Henry Coventry – is the grand front of the former Trocadero Restaurant, along with a number of quite fine Edwardian façades. In Oxenden Street the architectural character changes with a varied run of smaller-scale buildings at its southern end, becoming large and bland on its western angle with Coventry Street.

The theatre is the second on the site; the first opened on 18 January 1884 as the Prince's Theatre, designed by C. J. Phipps for actor–manager Edgar Bruce as part of a larger, unified scheme embracing the Thistle Hotel (originally Prince's Hotel and Restaurant), and fronting onto Whitcomb Street. In accordance with the overall concept of a coherent group of buildings, the architecture of the Prince's Hotel was extended to embrace the theatre frontage to Coventry Street, curving into Oxenden Street in a simplified form. In 1886 the theatre's name was changed to the Prince of Wales.

In 1937 the theatre's character changed dramatically, when the existing structure, considered old-fashioned, was demolished and a new one built, with a much more capacious auditorium. On 16 January the curtain came down on the final show, *Encore les Dames*, and on 17 June Gracie Fields laid the foundation stone of the new building, designed by the highly respected cinema architect Robert Cromie. The 1937 building, revealed to the theatre's public on 27 October that year with the first performance of *Les Folies de Paris et Londres*, is far removed from Phipps's archetypal three-tier, cream and gold auditorium, with its Moorish style ancillary rooms and staircases. The steel-framed structure with its artificial stone cladding sits uneasily against the earlier hotel, with the sawn-through junction just a little too ill-mannered. The corner tower, with its

ABOVE Altered in the early 1960s, Robert Cromie's auditorium has a lilac, grey and gold colour scheme.

RIGHT The corner tower of the Prince of Wales Theatre, as seen from Coventry Street, sits above the main theatre entrance. Once crowned with a flagstaff and decorated with neon lights, the tower was an eye-catching landmark.

long, curving, cantilevered canopy, echoes the original; the open corner drum should be outlined in neon, and it should also have a crowning flagstaff.

Internally, the building is vaguely archaeological: although it is much altered, parts of Cromie's design can be identified in, for example, the cocktail bar and parts of the American Bar; the most complete survival is the stalls bar, which retains its dance floor and bar counter fashioned in backlit glass blocks. The foyer is relatively plain, with typical Art Deco reeded and recessed lighting channels, and Cromie's auditorium, detrimentally altered in the early 1960s, now has a lilac, grey and gold colour scheme, introduced for *Aspects of Love* in the early 1990s.

A joy in this theatre is a collection of framed playbills, lovingly assembled by the present manager, Mike Churchill, and exhibited mainly in the stalls bar. Other theatres exhibit playbills, but almost without exception they are undated. Each one on show here is accurately dated, multiplying considerably the pleasure of examining them. Here are *Sweet Charity*, 1967, with Juliet Prowse; *Harvey*, 1975, starring James Stewart; *South Pacific*, 1988, with Gemma Craven; *What a Show*, 1995, with Tommy Steele – and many, many more.

QUEEN'S THEATRE
SHAFTESBURY AVENUE

HISTORY

• 1907. Designed by W. G. R. Sprague and opened on 8 October.

• 1940. Bombed and badly damaged in air raid of 24 September.

• 1959. Reopened following rebuilding and remodelling.

• Statutorily Listed Historic Building: Grade II.

OF SPECIAL INTEREST

• W. G. R. Sprague's auditorium.

• Rebuilt front of house by Bryan Westwood of Westwood Sons and Partners in consultation with Sir Hugh Casson.

• Seating capacity: 990.

ABOVE A bronze cast of the mask of Comedy decorates an entrance door from the remodelled theatre.

RIGHT Exterior of 1957 by Bryan Westwood of Westwood Sons and Partners with Sir Hugh Casson.

O n Tuesday, 24 September 1940, 110 enemy aircraft carried out a night raid on London, dropping large numbers of incendiary bombs, mainly north of the River Thames. Although the attack was somewhat random, the Queen's was hit by a high explosive device which destroyed the front of house, and with it W. G. R. Sprague's fine, almost symmetrical, Edwardian Renaissance composition which mirrored the Gielgud (formerly the Globe) to its south. A photograph hanging in the present foyer shows a Corinthian-columned vestibule with an impressive geometrical Imperial staircase. It may be that one day the loss will be rectified, perhaps with the help of Arts Council or National Lottery funding.

It was not until 1957 that the work of rebuilding and remodelling commenced, the scheme being designed by architect Bryan Westwood of

Westwood, Sons and Partners in consultation with Sir Hugh Casson, who had been Director of Architecture for the 1951 Festival of Britain. The new work clearly reflects the spirit of its age: a five-storey curving curtain-wall structure, in a commercial grey-blue brick and casement-window office style. The foyer, stalls and circle bars, with their deeply reeded walls and dark wood, are spacious extensions of the mid-1950s street architecture, as is the grand staircase with its enormous timber handrail. The theatre was reopened on 8 July 1959 by John Gielgud in a Shakespearean recital, *The Seven Ages of Man*. Externally, the long, red-brick, 12-bay flank elevation overlooks the remains of St Anne's Church (1686), also bombed in 1940 and probably designed by William Talman, who later worked at Burghley House, Stamford, and Chatsworth, Derbyshire.

Just as at the Lyric Theatre, Hammersmith, in west London, where modern offices encase Frank Matcham's resited and elevated auditorium, so at the Queen's the magic of the auditorium is enhanced by the contrast with the pared-down architecture of the late 1950s. Sprague's interior, which survived the bombing almost undamaged, is a controlled, exquisite composition in what was described as the Old Italian Renaissance style, incorporating two cantilevered balconies decorated in an Adamesque manner, and three tiers of boxes either side of a rectangular framed proscenium. The more baroque saucer-domed ceiling has four semi-circular lunettes, each adorned with pairs of seated muses. The decorative scheme when the theatre opened on 8 October 1907 was cream and gold, and these colours predominate in the auditorium almost a century later. Skeletal remains of original timber stage machinery are extant in a single corner trap, a grave trap and an upstage bridge.

J. E. Vedrenne, the first lessee, named his theatre after Queen Alexandra. The first production was Madeline Ryley's *The Sugar Bowl*, followed more successfully by *The Devil's Disciple*. Other successes followed, including *Potash and Perlmutter* (1914), *The Apple Cart* (1929, with Cedric Hardwicke and Edith Evans), *Private Lives* (1972), and a revival of *Hair* (1974).

ROYAL COURT
THEATRE
SLOANE SQUARE

HISTORY

• 1870. Converted chapel on south side of Sloane Square opens as New Chelsea Theatre, soon to be renamed Belgravia Theatre.

• 1887. Belgravia Theatre demolished.

• 1888. Royal Court Theatre rebuilt to the designs of Walter Emden and Bertie Crewe on the east side of Sloane Square.

• 1934. Theatre converted to cinema use by architect Cecil Masey.

• 1940. Theatre and adjacent underground station damaged in bombing raid.

• 1952. London Theatres Guild commissions architect Robert Cromie to rehabilitate the building.

• 1994. Scheme of rebuilding and repair initiated. Works begin 1996.

• 2000. Theatre reopened.

• Statutorily Listed Historic Building: Grade II.

OF SPECIAL INTEREST

• An outstanding scheme, combining selective retention of original fabric with imaginative planning and design within fixed limits, by architects Haworth Tomkins.

• Seating capacity: 400.

ABOVE Exposed original riveted ironwork in the auditorium.

OPPOSITE The red-brick and stone sressed front of 1888 has been given a more up-to-date look as part of the latest modernization scheme with the introduction of fully glazed doors and a bracketed open metal balcony.

ow lying in Chelsea Old Church graveyard, Sir Hans Sloane was a physician and astute man of letters; not only did he buy the Lordship of the Manor of Chelsea, he was also elected President of the Royal Society, an honour he shares with no lesser figures than Sir Christopher Wren, Samuel Pepys and Sir Isaac Newton. In 1717 – maybe through some artful manoeuvring, given the disparity in social class between the families – he married his daughter Elizabeth to Charles Cadogan, the exceedingly wealthy heir to the neighbouring Cadogan Estate. A copy of a fine statue of Sir Hans by Michael Rysbrack (1737), originally in the Chelsea Physics Garden, stands at the western end of the square that bears his name, along with a bronze fountain by Gilbert Ledward (1951) and, at the east end, an isolated war memorial, all three set in an arid York stone paved desert.

At the beginning of the 18th century Chelsea was comparatively rural, and even 100 years later the area that now comprises Sloane Square was little more than an enclosed semi-natural open space. Inevitably, as London expanded buildings sprang up, including a dissenters' chapel on the south side of the square. Unable to muster and retain a large enough congregation, the chapel fell empty during the 1860s, to be reopened in 1870 as the New Chelsea Theatre. Not eminently successful, the theatre was renamed The Belgravia and remodelled at the end of the year by architect Walter Emden for the manageress, Marie Litton. By 1887 the character of the area was changing dramatically, and over the next 10 years it would take on a persona much resembling the modern townscape. To facilitate the remodelling of the Square the theatre was demolished, and a new building, designed by Walter Emden and Bertie Crewe, was erected on its east side, opening as the Royal Court Theatre on 24 September 1888.

The red-brick and stone front of four storeys and three main bays, in the Italian Renaissance style, has a central pediment and applied Corinthian columns to the upper storey. The outer bays are enlivened by richly carved cambered pediments representing the Arts and Drama, and new main entrance doors have been inserted under a modern balcony as part of the latest refurbishment. To the north of the theatre is an ornate brick and stucco building of 1899, while to its south is a despairingly grey curtain-walled block rising above the underground station, which, along with the theatre, was bombed with considerable loss of life in 1940.

In 1934 the Royal Court closed its doors on live theatre, reopening as a cinema after alterations by architect Cecil Masey. At that time Masey was linked with the Granada super-cinema circuit, working with the flamboyant Russian-born interior designer Theodore Komissarjevsky, and in an international modern style with Reginald Uren. Following the wartime bomb damage, nothing was done by way of fabric repair until 1952, when the London Theatre Guild commissioned Robert Cromie, a respected cinema architect, to rehabilitate the building. Further works were undertaken in 1956, and again in 1964.

It seems that the theatre was built with a sense of adventure embedded in its structure. Here it was that many of George Bernard Shaw's plays were first produced, including *Major Barbara* (1905) and *Heartbreak House* (1921). John

ABOVE The drum wall, seen here in the dress-circle bar, extends through the height of the building.

LEFT It is very much a matter of personal choice whether the rather stark structural ironwork above the dress circle sits well in the context of the altered Empire-style auditorium.

ABOVE A stroke of genius has created the intimate basement-level restaurant, absorbing ladies' public lavatories that once served Sloane Square.

Osborne's *Look Back In Anger* (1956), and Arnold Wesker's *Roots* (1959) and *Chips With Everything* (1962) were among other modern distinguished firsts. Today, new works are the hallmark of the Royal Court.

By 1994 the theatre had, following many years of under-funded maintenance and cut-price rehabilitation, reached a point where a serious assessment of its future needed to be made, doubtless against the inevitable lure of the site's redevelopment value. By coincidence, it was at this time that the National Lottery was born, an innovation that was to prove a crucial lifeline for the Court. In-house meetings with design consultants, Theatre Projects, produced a short list of architectural practices that could provide not only efficient resuscitation, but also the additional flair, sympathy and inspiration to make a commonplace solution special.

A brave decision was taken to appoint a young practice, Haworth Tomkins, and at completion it has proved to be justified. Following the submission of a feasibility study, a grant of £18.8 million was awarded by the Arts Council towards the creation of a functional, up-to-date theatre space within existing site boundaries and behind the original front wall. It was decided to retain the Emden–Crewe auditorium and, quite surprisingly, the proscenium arch. The remainder of the theatre has been replanned, including a daring but successful excavation under the Square to form a basement restaurant, taking in the former Sloane Square ladies' public lavatories. Also within the envelope are the tremendously successful Jerwood Studio Theatres, Upstairs and Downstairs.

The remodelled Royal Court is flexible and tightly planned, without for a moment losing its grip on its original identity. The architects have been eminently successful in maintaining a sense of history in an obviously forward-thinking brief, and they have applied an 'archaeology meets high-tech' approach to the front-of-house areas. The treatment of exposed original yellow stock brickwork in an Ancient Monuments manner, abutting raw concrete walls, may, however, stand a better chance of being understood if information boards or discreet labelling were provided. Loving touches, such as the retention of the rediscovered mosaic floor to the foyer, with its flowered black, green and apricot edging, should not go unremarked. The loss of the timber stage machinery, which had miraculously survived the bomb damage is regrettable but inevitable. However, in a world where 'regulations' have become an architect's worst nightmare, this project is a tribute to both faith and flair.

ROYAL NATIONAL THEATRE

UPPER GROUND

OF SPECIAL INTEREST

• The National Theatre as a major public building, and as a powerful dramatic entity.

• Seating capacity: Olivier 1,100; Lyttleton 900; Cottesloe 200–350.

ABOVE A geometric composition of the modern utilitarian seating that serves 350 theatre-goers in the small Cottesloe Theatre.

RIGHT The Olivier – grand, dark, shuttered concrete – is heavily reliant on lighting banks, and has a flexible acting area ironically employing 'old-fashioned' trolleys.

harles Dickens, a tireless walker and astute observer of London life, would almost certainly have been unable to resist the magnetic attraction of a relatively new Thames crossing. Waterloo Bridge, originally Strand Bridge, designed by Sir John Rennie and opened in 1817 by the Prince Regent, would have provided the author with the perfect platform from which to absorb the myriad downstream sights and sounds he would weave into the wonderful opening paragraphs of *Bleak House* (1852) and *Our Mutual Friend* (1864).

As he leaned on the parapet, the superb 600-foot-long river façade of Sir William Chambers's Somerset House (1786) would have dominated the north riverbank, just as it does today; but there would have remained space for the grand west wing, fronting onto the bridge approach, which was to be designed by Sir James Pennethorne and begun in 1851. Dickens was a lifelong lover of the theatre, and at this time might well have been mulling over the embryonic suggestions of publisher Effingham Wilson, made around 1848, for the establishment of a national theatre. It was a project Dickens would support, but in the event nothing would be achieved before his death in 1870. On the south bank Dickens would see, in a smoky murk, the dim outlines of mills, breweries, sawmills and lead works, each with its individual wharf or dock, fronting rows of small artisans' dwellings. He could not know that here, almost exactly 100 years later, on 13 July 1951, the year of the Festival of Britain, Her Majesty the Queen would lay the foundation stone for the National Theatre, dedicated to the living memory of William Shakespeare, on a site adjacent to the Royal Festival Hall provided by the London County Council.

RIGHT Grey shuttered concrete forms the fabric of both exterior and interior at the National, but the circulation and restaurant areas are lively in their variety of shapes and views: not always harmonious, but always interesting.

The laying of the foundation stone was, for the many individuals and organizations involved with the creation of a National Theatre – in particular Sir Laurence Olivier and Oliver Lyttleton – the culmination of years of what must at times have been depressing negotiations and discussions on many levels. As time moved on further problems arose: by the early 1960s the promised government monies had failed to materialize, and by necessity the Old Vic became the National Theatre's temporary home.

Nevertheless, plans for the new building continued. Although at the millennium Denys Lasdun often stands condemned by conservationists as a founding father of comprehensive redevelopment, his selection as architect to the scheme at the critical juncture in 1963 was inspirational, for, probably alone among British architects of that time, he had the ability to produce a scheme of worldwide significance.

The original proposal included an opera house (an element not dropped until 1967), intended to replace Sadler's Wells. In drawing up his sketch designs for the two buildings, Lasdun must have been acutely aware of their juxtaposition to Somerset House and to the arching visual link of Sir Giles Gilbert Scott's second Waterloo Bridge, completed in 1942, producing a contrasting composition of sculptural multi-layered brutalism which he would retain in his final scheme. On its completion in 1976, it was very easy for prominent figures to condemn the concrete geometry of the building, its massing and sense of place; but a quarter of a century on it stands as a living tribute to Lasdun's genius.

Slightly hemmed in by the sheer, stone-faced east wall to the southern Waterloo Bridge approach, which masks the Queen Elizabeth Hall on its western side, external walkways are linked on an almost square plan to exhibition spaces and restaurants, in turn accessed from paired full-height foyers serving the Olivier and Lyttleton auditoria. The whole is crowned by two large, unadorned, flat-roofed fly towers which seem to emphasize the cascading horizontality of the composition as it sits above the river. In addition to the two major spaces, the Cottesloe, a studio theatre, almost abandoned in the early design stages in order to save money,

LEFT View from the riverfront (northwest). Denys Lasdun's layered composition is dominated by twin fly-towers.

provides a remarkably flexible three-dimensional courtyard arena. Inside, it is a black box with multiple lighting banks, black walls, brown carpets and utility seating for an audience of up to 350.

The Olivier, with its pictorial open stage and single balcony, seats 1,100 and is the largest of the three theatres, shuttered concrete emphasizing its grand, dark ambience. With brown carpets and mauve seating, much reliance is again placed on the use of multiple lighting banks.

Although the Lyttleton, having 900 seats, has been designed with a conventional proscenium, the use of shuttered sculptured concrete with dark brown seats and floor coverings again leaves the lighting to do much work. The theatre's design has about it more than a hint of film.

Success has not been in short supply at the

National. The year 1980 saw Sir Michael Gambon dominate Brecht's *Life of Galileo*, and in the same year Mary Whitehouse and Sir Horace Cutler threatened prosecution for obscenity over *The Romans in Britain*. In 1982 *Guys and Dolls* was a smash hit, as was *The Wind in the Willows* in 1990, 1991, 1993 and 1994. Dame Judi Dench was to win the Olivier award for best actress in 1995 for *Absolute Hell* and *A Little Night Music*. In 1997 the National's productions won six of seven possible Evening Standard Awards.

In 1976 the *Architectural Review* acclaimed the National Theatre as 'London's most exciting new building', and that accolade has stood the test of time. The building stands as a lasting memorial to its architect, Sir Denys Lasdun, who died on 11 January 2001.

ROYAL OPERA HOUSE
COVENT GARDEN

OF SPECIAL INTEREST

• The premier opera house in Great
Britain. Architecturally distinguished both
as an historic building and as a world-
class arts venue at the opening of the
21st century.

• Seating capacity: 2,160.

ABOVE A symbol
of the great
beauty that
suffuses the whole
of this building.

OPPOSITE Part
elevation showing
the restored Floral
Hall (1858–60)
by Edward M.
Barry and the
main façade to
the Royal Opera
House (1857–8)
fronting onto
Bow Street.

he Royal Opera House lies less than a mile to the west of Londinium, which fell into serious decline with the collapse of the Roman Empire in the late 4th century AD. Superseding the city at the end of the 6th century AD, Saxon Lundenwic flourished in the area of Aldwych, the Strand and Covent Garden. It was with the aid of Royal Opera House monies that the Museum of London carried out an exhaustive and rewarding archaeological excavation on part of its two-acre site in 1996, prior to the commencement of rebuilding works, which revealed an important centre of international trade and commerce.

During the medieval period the land reverted to partially enclosed pasture, owned by the great Benedictine Abbey of St Peter, Westminster – hence the name Covent Garden, which derives from 'convent garden'. In the mid-17th century the flower and vegetable market arrived to occupy the piazza created in the 1630s by Inigo Jones.

Theatrical performances were suppressed during the Commonwealth (1649–60), but at the restoration of the monarchy Charles II granted two letters patent licensing the recipients to operate theatrical companies. The first was granted to the Poet Laureate William D'Avenant and his Duke's Company (named for D'Avenant's patron, the Duke of York), on 15 January 1662, and the second to Thomas Killigrew and his King's Company, on 25 April 1662. Thus was created a virtual joint monopoly on dramatic performances in London. D'Avenant's patent was obviously of immense value, and by 1714, after being sold on, was in the ownership of the famous harlequin and virtual inventor of pantomime, John Rich, who opened his Lincoln's Inn Fields Theatre that same year. Having struggled to make ends meet over the intervening 14 years, by extreme good fortune Rich found financial success with his first staging of John Gay's *The Beggar's Opera* in 1728, and with his new-found wealth decided to build a grand theatre to upstage Drury Lane, on a plot he leased in Covent Garden in 1731.

The site occupied the northeast angle of Jones's piazza, which was by this time somewhat less than socially desirable and hemmed in by houses and shops. Edward Shepherd, Rich's architect at Lincoln's Inn Fields and creator of Shepherd Market in Mayfair, was commissioned to build the new theatre, which he did in the stock Georgian tradition, utilizing a rectangular fanned auditorium with pit benches, three tiers of boxes to the sides, and boxes and two galleries to the rear. John Rich saw his theatre open, but died in 1761, whereupon control passed to the superlative administrator Thomas Harris, who in 1791 engaged Henry Holland (the partner of Capability Brown) to remodel the auditorium incorporating a proscenium stage.

On 20 September 1808 the building burnt down, and a replacement, entered from Bow Street through a solid Grecian portico, was designed by Sir Robert Smirke, architect of the British Museum. To finance the expensive new building, admission prices were raised by 6d and 1s, sparking off 67 days of what became known as the 'Old Price' riots. In the 1840s opera was established in the theatre following the arrival of Michael Costa and his company of singers from Her Majesty's Theatre, which they had left after a row. As a result the building had to be brought into line with European opera houses, and for this task the slightly

new Korean Airlines headquarters in Seoul (above) brings maintenance and
nagement together. The roof truss (facing page, bottom) was assembled on the
und and then hoisted to the roof. The double top chord (facing page, top)
ne bow arch straddles the supporting box columns.

complex and the only one of its kind in the world. "It's not an affec-
ion; it's a moment diagram realized three dimensionally," explains
lliam Baker, partner in charge of structural engineering for the pro-
t. Twin bow arches beginning at opposite, outside corners of the rec-
gle converge at a 4-by-4-foot box column located against the office
lding at the midpoint of the rectangle. In the same way a balancing
e helps a tightrope walker maintain equilibrium, concave rib trusses
either side of the bow arch form balanced cantilevers that support
roof, and span to the front of the hangar on one side of the arch and
he rear wall from the other. The dead loads of the cantilevers consist
he ribs themselves, the bridging members that run perpendicular to
ribs, and the metal cladding.

The wind loads acting on the roof are handled in an adroit inver-
n of Bernoulli's principle, which describes how airplanes fly. Air
ves faster over the curved surface on the top of an airplane's wing
n the flat surface underneath. Slow-moving air exerts a higher pres-
e on a surface than fast-moving air; consequently, the pressure
neath the wing is higher than that on top and pushes the wing
ward. By contrast, the hangar roof resembles an upside-down airfoil.
severe storms, winds can create suction strong enough to tear off a
f. This risk of uplift is reduced considerably with the bowl form
ause the forces are downward.

The massive truss, nearly 54 feet from the top cord of the bow to the
tom ties, was assembled on the ground. Using hydraulic strand jacks,
kers hoisted the roof at a rate of about one foot per hour. At 10 feet
ve the ground, the truss was allowed to assume its own weight and
bilize. At this stage, the standing metal seam cladding was installed
the hoisting continued until the top, about 92 feet above grade. It may
he literal interpretation of a moment diagram, but as an architectural
n it rolls with a grace that belies its vastness and makes it seem to
er effortlessly—a fitting image for an airline. ∎

Royal Debacle

The British press offers no
grace period, as officials of
the Royal Opera House (ROH)
in London's Covent Garden
learned this past winter.

In December, the 142-year-
old ROH reopened to the
public after a $500 million, 30-
month renovation led by the
London firm Jeremy Dixon
Edward Jones. Patrons soon
griped about poor site lines
and box-office bottlenecks,
but the biggest problems were
onstage, caused by bugs
in new software designed to
move sets. In the end, when
backdrops and other sceno-
graphic elements wouldn't
budge, a dozen performances
had to be canceled. Midway
through one performance, a
trapdoor failed to open, keeping an evil knight from making
his dramatic entrance. The
confused audience—and
onstage performers—waited
40 minutes before a flustered
ROH employee walked out of
the wings to apologize.

The London papers had a
field day. The *Guardian* called
the new ROH a "seemingly
endless roll call of disasters."
The *Telegraph*'s Norman
Lebrecht found problems
everywhere—onstage as well
as in the public-address system ("strident and hectoring")
and the men's bathrooms (not
enough hooks, so "jackets are
dumped on the floor"). "These
were the teething problems
you would expect from any
project of this size," says
Jeremy Dixon, one of the lead
architects. "But the ROH
is seen as a privileged institu-
tion, and thus becomes an
automatic target." *C.H.*

ABOVE Splendid, daunting, wonderful, frightening – adjectives applicable to Barry's auditorium depending, probably, on whether one is a performer or a member of the audience. *The Survey of London* (1970) called it 'the most beautiful auditorium in Great Britain', and few would dissent. Elliptical arches and pendentives support the saucer-domed ceiling.

dubious figure of Mr Benedict Albano was hired to remodel the auditorium once more, providing six tiers of boxes. The duly reconfigured theatre reopened as the Royal Italian Opera House in 1847; but the fates were again unkind, and it burnt down on 5 March 1856.

The architect commissioned to rebuild the theatre yet again was 26-year-old Edward M. Barry, son of Sir Charles Barry, the designer of the Palace of Westminster (1835–60), and he rose to the occasion with a very beautiful neo-Palladian fireproof structure which opened on 15 May 1858. Designed on a horseshoe plan, boxes – pit, grand and first tier – enclosed the pit and pit stalls, above which were amphitheatre stalls and side galleries. It was a layout especially advantageous for those who wanted to see and to be seen. Adjacent to the new building, Barry provided a graceful Italianate cast-iron Winter Garden annex for his opera house. Although the so-

LEFT Part of the design brief for the restoration and development of the Royal Opera House was that the lot of the Royal Ballet should be improved. This has been achieved with top-lit studios of uncommon quality and elegance.

ABOVE Horseshoe tiers are raised above a lower box tier in this very European theatre. The relievo above the proscenium arch (1858) is by Raffaelle Monti, who was perhaps better known as a sculptor. The stage set was designed by Semyon Pastukh and is from the Kirov Opera's production of *Otello*.

called Floral Hall was badly damaged by fire in 1956, it has been carefully restored to enhance the present-day renovated complex with additional circulation space. A new, uncompromising block to the south of the Floral Hall has been visually disengaged by the introduction of a fully glazed escalator enclosure, an architectural manoeuvre common in restoration work on historic buildings.

In 1900 Edwin O. Sachs, an authority on safe theatre design, installed an Asphaleia system of five hydraulically operated iron bridges, which formed a permanent stage floor. Above this the stage was counterweighted with a cyclorama and thunder run, in situ in the 1970s. All have since been removed, a serious loss in terms of theatre history, but fully justified in terms of the 21st-century site redevelopment, which has created a wonderful self-contained theatre village that incorporates elements ranging from ballet studios and craft departments to run-of-

the-mill administration and finance departments. Two studio theatres, the Linbury (seating 420) and the Clore (seating 200), have been designed into the complex. The architects for this scheme were Jeremy Dixon, Edward Jones and Charles Broughton, and to find fault with their work would be pernickety in the extreme. Nothing can be said in a short piece that will do adequate justice to their achievement, but Marcus Binney found the appropriate phrase when he wrote, 'From the moment you step through the doors you will be enthralled.'

SADLER'S WELLS
THEATRE
ROSEBERY AVENUE

OF SPECIAL INTEREST

• The evolution of Sadler's Wells from
its origins in 1683, through its various
metamorphoses, to the emergence of the
present building, opened in 1998.

• Seating capacity: 1,578;
Lilian Baylis Theatre 220.

ABOVE A pleasant
corner in the
circle bar – a
perfect place
for refreshment
pre-performance
or during the
interval.

ichard Sadler, Surveyor of the Highways, lived a comfortable late 17th-century life in rural Clerkenwell, his two-storey detached house surrounded by a large, well-treed garden, hinting at the possibility of profitable interests beyond his day job. In an area known up to the 16th century for its healing wells, Sadler discovered to his delight that he had on his land a chalybeate spring once owned by the medieval Hospital of St John, Clerkenwell, the head house of the Knights Hospitallers in England. A born entrepreneur, Sadler set out immediately to market his iron-infused water – with considerable, almost instantaneous success, comparable with the modern bottled mineral water phenomenon. So impressive was his strategy that hypochondriacs, including members of the royal family, flocked to Clerkenwell; but so did imitators. To fend off the competition, Sadler imported live entertainment – music, pageantry, fireworks and dancing – similar to that at fashionable Vauxhall Gardens, south of the River Thames, for the amusement of his clientèle. Sadler's so-called Musick House, later to become picturesquely known as New Tunbridge Wells, grew into a typical seven-bay, two-storey country house with up-to-date sashed windows under a steeply pitched tile roof. Sadler's wooden 'theatre', where the entertainments were presented, survived in the grounds until the mid-18th century, by which time public interest had waned and the audience had become disreputable.

In 1765 Thomas Rosoman bought the property and rebuilt the wooden 'theatre' in more substantial masonry in what were, by this time, less tranquil surroundings, and in its revitalized form the theatre became well known for its burlesques and pantomimes. In 1804 the nearby New River was ingeniously channelled into the building for the staging of contemporary victorious naval battles. In the later 1840s the Chartist movement, an expression of an upsurge in working-class egalitarian feeling, gathered strength in London; with revolution in France along with economic depression and rampant cholera outbreaks at home, the Marseillaise was

RIGHT Dramatic foyer and circulation spaces, designed by local architectural practice Nicholas Hare Associates in conjunction with Renton Howard Wood Levine, rise behind a sheer glazed screen to Rosebery Avenue.

LEFT The problems of a severely restricted site and a design brief that requires the new building to be fitted into the skeleton of its predecessor are many. This is a high-tech theatre with a bank of lighting panels on each auditorium flank wall, and the fly-floor control is reduced to a single console. Carpenters can still be seen, though, making up rough frames backstage – a pleasantly human touch.

RIGHT The main front of the theatre, with its dramatic foyer glazing, faces onto Rosebery Avenue.

ABOVE This simply presented group of busts pays a deserved tribute to those who worked to secure the future of Sadler's Wells for generations to come.

remodelled, this time by architect Bertie Crewe, only to become a cinema and then to close in 1906.

The theatre's true salvation was not forthcoming until the Wells was taken over by Lilian Baylis in 1925 to run in tandem with her already flourishing Old Vic Theatre. She demolished the old building and in 1931 rebuilt on the site, commissioning architect F. G. M. Chancellor to carry out the work, which he did in a dour, unimaginative style. Under the distinguished direction of Ninette de Valois, opera and ballet gained momentum, and the 'North London Old Vic' emerged from the theatrical shadows. Success followed success, albeit erratically. In 1988 the Baylis Theatre was designed by architects Chamberlain, Powell and Bon, and in 1994 Ian Albury became chief executive. Two years later, under his inspired leadership, Chancellor's building was demolished to make way for a new theatre designed by Renton Howard Wood Levine, with Nicholas Hare Associates, which would be moulded into the skeletal fabric of the earlier building.

The inevitable problems associated with designing a new theatre in this way on a restricted site have been overcome at the Wells in a bold but severe solution. The cold silver-grey panelling of the fly-tower is offset by the dramatic foyer glazing and warm brickwork, beautifully laid in Flemish bond to the body of the building. The light and airy foyer levels are designed for multipurpose use, with rooms of varying sizes adjacent on each floor, thus offering the possibility of additional sources of finance (which are only too necessary).

Although the basic form of the structure has been maintained, the grid has been raised from 16 metres to 22 metres and the proscenium has been widened from 9 to 15 metres. The seating lacks luxury, and the preserving of earlier levels within the auditorium has caused sightlines to the rear of the stalls and first circle to be curtailed. Disabled access, though, has been carefully considered throughout the building.

So, here in Rosebery Avenue a dreary building has been swept away to be replaced by a theatre of the highest quality, where architectural aesthetics and technology have made a near-perfect marriage. Completing a very special ensemble is the pioneering Spa Green Estate of 1946–50, designed by international modernist architects Lubetkin and Skinner, while next door to the theatre is the impressive Metropolitan Water Board Building (1914–20) designed by H. Austen Hall. Enhancing the group is Thomas Rudge's *Angel of Victory* memorial close by in Spa Gardens.

And yes, Richard Sadler's well has been preserved – in the corridor at the back of the stalls!

heard to be played at Sadler's Wells in anticipation of a civil war that failed to materialize.

Although Shakespeare returned to the Wells after the passing of the Theatres Act in 1843, which broke the grip of the patent theatres, the venue was not popular; in fact, the term 'Sadler's Wells make-up' (consisting of limewash scrapings and dust) was an allusion to the theatre's poverty of resources. In the early 1870s new uses were proposed for the building, and in 1876 the New Spa Roller Skating Rink opened. Even after the interior had been remodelled by C. J. Phipps in 1879, the public stayed away. Music hall generated some response over the following decades, and in 1901 the building was again

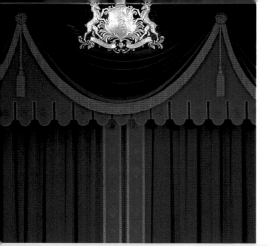

ST MARTIN'S THEATRE
WEST STREET

ABOVE The silver
and gold arms of
the Willoughby
de Broke family
set into the
proscenium.

RIGHT
The Adamesque
oval royal retiring
room, with, above
the chimney
piece, a delightful
painting of
Compton Verney,
Warwickshire, by
Frank Gaskell.

eparated from the New Ambassadors Theatre by the narrow Tower Court, and built three years later in 1916, St Martin's Theatre was designed by W. G. R. Sprague for Richard Grenville, 19th Baron Willoughby de Broke; Grenville's ancestral Warwickshire home, Compton Verney, lies in sweeping grasslands to the southeast of Charlecote Park, with its tenuous links to the young Shakespeare as a would-be poacher. Above the chimney piece in an oval Adamesque royal retiring room to the rear of the stalls is a small oil painting by Frank Gaskell which looks across a Capability Brown landscape of 1772 to the house. Sited in the Domesday village of Contone, deserted by 1461 to make way for sheep runs, much of the external fabric of the building was designed by Robert Adam (1760), but the rooms are surprisingly plain, a fact that may have some considerable bearing on the interior design of the theatre.

St Martin's covers much of its island site, originally occupied by a group of 16 small buildings, and its four-storey classical ashlar façade dominates the more compact Ambassadors. At ground-floor level pairs of arched openings flank a wide central entrance, with upper-circle access on the extreme right, all contained under a modern canopy. Giant engaged Ionic columns extend through three storeys, supporting a triglyph frieze, cornice and parapet. The *Architectural Review* in 1916 drew attention to a large bronzed central cartouche grouped with flags mounted on the parapet and vases supported on dies to either side, destroyed during the Second World War. Their replacement would put a dramatic finishing touch to the elevation.

Entered through three pairs of polished wood doors, complete with their original furniture, the pretty, symmetrical Adamesque foyer employs much

OPPOSITE The auditorium is of exceptionally high quality. Turned balusters to the serpentine box front of almost domestic scale contrast with the giant Doric engaged columns and piers – a fitting setting for Agatha Christie's *Mousetrap*.

ABOVE The part front elevation to St Martin's Theatre was once a dominant façade in West Street.

in spirit to Compton Verney, for here is all the missing classical domesticity of the great house, on a grand scale.

The dress circle is five rows deep and the upper circle eight, each behind close-balustered serpentine fronts. The superb polished walnut lining to this classical interior presents a slightly incongruous combination of considerable scale and the domestic theatre. Giant Doric engaged columns dominate the auditorium under a triglyph frieze and mutule cornice; the whole is crowned by a fine glazed circular domed ceiling within a dentilled surround. An eye-catching focal point within the proscenium arch is the silver and gold Willoughby de Broke coat of arms. A noticeable feature of the auditorium, meanwhile, is the welcome absence of lighting banks, which mar so many otherwise fine interiors. Wall coverings are a not unattractive pink with gold pattern.

A good dress-circle bar overlooking West Street has a series of *Mousetrap* cartoons lining its walls, commemorating the house's longest-running show.

Although late in date, the timber machinery contained under the stage is superb. A grave trap, corner traps, bridges and slotes survive in good condition in a deep cellar and mezzanine. The ensemble is to some extent damaged by an intrusive brick-built control room within the sub-stage area, but with care all could be restored. Flying is achieved by a combination of hemp and counterweighting.

St Martin's opened on 23 November 1916, with a performance of *Houp La!* produced by Frank Collins and directed by C. B. Cochran. John Galsworthy's *Sin Game* had an extended run in the early 1920s, and in 1921 *A Bill of Divorcement* established the exceptional quality of Meggie Albanesi, who was to die at the age of just 24, before she could reach her full potential. In 1925 *The Ghost Train* by Arnold Ridley ran for over 650 performances. *The Shop at Sly Corner* found success in 1945, and *Sleuth* ended its record run in 1974 when *The Mousetrap* was transferred from the Ambassadors Theatre. The world's longest-running play has been in St Martin's since that date, and looks set to run for some time to come.

marbling with gold highlighting to Ionic pilastered decoration under a single-panel ceiling. The main staircase to the right of the foyer is modest, but a very attractive plaque to actress Meggie Albanesi, who died on 9 December 1923, is displayed in the enclosure. Enter the auditorium and be transported

SAVOY THEATRE
STRAND

HISTORY

• 1881. Theatre designed by C. J. Phipps for Richard D'Oyly Carte.

• 1903. Extensive repair works, fireproofing and overhaul of heating and ventilation by architect A. Bloomfield Jackson.

• 1929. Theatre completely remodelled by Frank A. Tugwell, with interior decoration by Basil Ionides. Easton and Robertson alter the Savoy Court entrance.

• 1990. Building extensively damaged by fire.

• 1993. Restoration completed by Whitfield Partners and theatre reopens.

• Statutorily Listed
Historic Building: Grade II*.

OF SPECIAL INTEREST

• The planning of the theatre on its steeply sloping site.

• The superb mature Art Deco interior.

• Seating capacity: 1,156.

ABOVE Small but perfectly placed figure groups catch the eye in both the original and later foyers.

OPPOSITE Silver-leafed fluting to the balcony front and rear walls contrasts superbly with the giant wall panel of Chinese motif reliefs. A spectacularly successful exercise in the restrained use of colour and, in this instance, of restoration.

ngland was experiencing a protracted period of particularly warm but stormy weather when, in 1246, Henry III granted the land upon which the Savoy now stands – then the site of Simon de Montfort's palace – to Peter, Earl of Savoy and Richmond, for a rent of three barbed arrows to be delivered yearly to the Exchequer. Peter willed it in 1268 to the monastery of St Bernard Montjoux, Savoy, whose dependent house, the Hospital of Saints Nicholas and Barnard at Hornchurch, Essex, cared for the poor, aged and sick. Two years later the land was bought by Queen Eleanor of Castile, wife of King Edward I, who gifted it to her second son Edmund, Earl of Lancaster. By 1370 it had been completely rebuilt with unequalled magnificence by Edmund's grandson Henry, Duke of Lancaster.

Sadly, this magnificence was not to last – 1377 was the high point in the short-lived Peasants' Revolt, and Wat Tyler's rebels duly destroyed the sumptuous palace. The site then languished in ruins until 1505, when it was rebuilt, upon the instruction of King Henry VII, as the Savoy Hospital, which provided nightly accommodation for 100 poor people. To the rear of the Hospital, the chapel of St John the Baptist (now known as the Queen's Chapel of the Savoy) was built in 1510; the chapel survives within the serene setting of its grassy graveyard.

Following the closure of the hospital in 1702, the buildings began to deteriorate. Nevertheless, a protracted land-ownership dispute ensued between the Crown and the Duchy of Lancaster which eventually resulted in a land-share agreement in 1772. In 1816, the site was cleared to accommodate the new Waterloo Bridge approach road. The Savoy site was helped to prominence by the Victoria Embankment, which was begun in 1864. This enhanced the setting of all buildings along the Strand and improved access along the riverfront.

In 1881, on the Savoy site, which was by now covered with small buildings grouped around Fountain Court and Beaufort Buildings, construction work started on the Savoy Theatre. The work was put in hand by Richard D'Oyly Carte, who since 1877 had been manager of the Opera Comique, adjacent to the Globe Theatre in Wych Street, now Aldwych. The Savoy was D'Oyly Carte's first theatre; his success had begun when, in 1875, he produced Gilbert and Sullivan's *Trial By Jury* at the Royalty Theatre. His fortunes with Gilbert and Sullivan continued when, in 1878, *HMS Pinafore* opened and then ran for 700 nights, followed by *The Pirates of Penzance* (1880) and *Patience* (1881), by which time Gilbert and Sullivan were D'Oyly Carte's partners and his profits were soaring.

On the back of these profits, D'Oyly Carte commissioned C. J. Phipps in 1881 to design his own Savoy Theatre. Phipps came up with an Italian Renaissance design, overcoming in his plans the problems posed by the steep site by positioning his main entrance on the angle between Carting Lane and Savoy Way. Always forward-looking, D'Oyly Carte was proud to unveil the theatre as the first public building in the world to be totally illuminated by electricity, which would enhance the white, yellow and gold décor. As a precaution against power failure, however, the gas pilot lights would be kept lit!

In 1884 D'Oyly Carte decided to build a hotel next to his theatre. This time

ABOVE A fully armed golden knight, echoing the medieval origins of the site, crowns the main entrance to the Savoy complex, against the backdrop of Collcutt's hotel building.

he engaged architect T. E. Collcutt, who would later design his Palace Theatre – part of the expanding D'Oyly Carte empire – in 1891. The hotel was the beginning of what was to become an even larger complex, which grew in stages.

In 1903 Savoy Court – the short approach road to the theatre and the hotel from the Strand – was refronted to match the hotel, and a new theatre entrance and extensive alterations to the auditorium and foyer were put in hand. The west block was added in 1905 and the Embankment block in 1910. The *Building News* of 22 January 1904 refers to extensive alterations being demanded by London County Council to meet the ever more comprehensive building and fire regulations, and to

a decorative scheme in Venetian red, old gold and peacock blue.

By 1929 the three-tier auditorium was considered old-fashioned, and architect Frank A. Tugwell was commissioned to rebuild the theatre practically from scratch. All that remained after the demolition works were Phipps's Carting Lane entrance and the main side walls into which Tugwell designed his two-tier auditorium, with interior decoration by designer Basil Ionides. Levels within the building are governed by the sloping site: Savoy Court corresponds with the upper-circle level, and the scenery get-in from Carting Lane is at fly-floor level, an inconvenience that makes for some manoeuvring difficulties. At the same time as

RIGHT Powerful, beautifully sculpted horned bronze horses are used with dramatic effect on the entrance doors from Savoy Court.

BELOW A quiet corner, embodying the atmosphere of the 1930s.

Tugwell was engaged on the auditorium, modernist architects Easton and Robertson, who were later to design the fine laboratory buildings adjacent to the Sadler's Wells Theatre, were employed to modernize the Savoy Court elevation. They installed a range of glazed doors framed in stylized drapes, within a polished stainless-steel canopy supporting the theatre name in oversized steel sans-serif letters, set against the Doulton Carrara Ware (similar to faience) facing to the hotel. Beyond the doors lies the mirrored foyer with its silver-leafed rectangles, a pretty box office and a staircase that descends to the stalls and the dress circle. This is the visitor's first glimpse of Ionides' inspired Art Deco *moderne* interior.

The two-tier auditorium, decorated like the foyer in silver-leafed rectangles, is a tribute to the creativity of Basil Ionides and is one of the great examples of Art Deco interior design. The front half of the auditorium has two giant sounding boards either side of the plain proscenium, each designed to accommodate 43 decorated panels derived from a Chinese lacquer screen, but designed in a contrived perspective. Behind, the walls are heavily fluted, producing a remarkable display of graded light and shade, with tongued fluting extending along the balcony fronts. The ceiling above the stalls houses rectangular lighting panels, and above the upper circle a cloudy blue sky has been painted. Colour is used sparingly on the sunken ornamental soffit panels to the underside of the balconies, as an eye-catching contrast to the expanses of silver leaf.

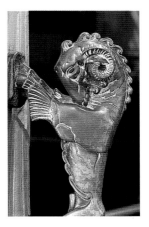

Stand at the front of the stalls, look back into this auditorium and imagine the devastation left by a totally destructive fire in 1990. The ceiling was open to the sky and the decoration virtually destroyed. With a dedication far beyond the normal, the management, along with the architects Whitfield Partners, set about a restoration of breathtaking quality – comparable to the refurbishment of Castle Howard, Yorkshire, or Upark, Sussex, after equally extensive fire damage – and one which everyone who visits the theatre is able to appreciate. The building reopened in 1993.

Sadly, nothing remains of the original timber stage machinery. Instead, a state-of-the-art modular counterweighted stage has been installed and the grid has been lowered to accommodate the hotel's swimming pool above.

Many of the Savoy's greatest stage moments were during the years 1910–18, when Henry Irving was actor–manager. Irving would appear regularly on stage, and prior to his death, James Montgomery's farce *Nothing But the Truth* was to run for close on 600 performances. Following this, after Gilbert and Sullivan revivals in the early 1930s, *The Man Who Came to Dinner* ran for over 700 performances in 1942. *The Secretary Bird* ran for 1,500 performances ending in 1972, followed by the highly successful *Noises Off* (1,912 performances).

SHAFTESBURY
THEATRE
SHAFTESBURY AVENUE

ABOVE Within the tympanum, above the boxes to stage right, sit life-size figures representing Music and Poetry. The painted roundel depicts a rural scene.

t Giles High Street curves gently away from St Giles Circus and Centre Point for about a quarter of a mile to become High Holborn, where once three theatres stood: the Duke's (burnt down 1880), the Holborn (closed 1887) and the Empire (bombed 1941). The High Street, bypassed since the mid-19th century by New Oxford Street, traces the line of the north boundary wall to the 12th-century Leper Hospital of St Giles, fanning out as it reaches High Holborn to take the form of a medieval marketplace. The hospital chapel was demolished in the aftermath of the dissolution of the monasteries (1539), and the present – very beautiful – Portland-stone church of St Giles-in-the-Fields, designed by the Palladian Henry Flitcroft, architect of Woburn Abbey, was consecrated in 1733. It was here that actor–manager David Garrick of the Theatre Royal, Drury Lane, married Eva Marie Violetti in 1749.

The Shaftesbury Theatre is sited on the eastern angle between Shaftesbury Avenue and High Holborn, some 200 yards to the east of the church. In 1640 the English divine and poet George Herbert wrote, 'No sooner is a temple built to God, but the Devil builds a chapel close by,' a sentiment echoed in August 1838 by the young Mary Anne Evans – later to write magnificently as George Eliot – who in those early days considered the theatre to be sinful. So it is that St-Giles-in-the-Fields is destined to keep a benevolent watch on the more wayward late arrival. Between the two is a series of dull blocks including, in particular, Endeavour House, accompanied by an excess of concrete paving and young trees. Buildings of interest, if not of great moment, close to the theatre include Alton House with its glazed modern façade and the local council's own Berkshire House.

As is so often the case, in order to build the theatre a small block of run-down properties, including a pub, had to be demolished. The developers were Walter and Frederick Melville, whose Popular Playhouse Ltd would present melodrama at the New Prince's Theatre (as the Shaftesbury was first known) when it opened on 26 December 1911 with a presentation of *The Three Musketeers*. The architect commissioned to design the building was Bertie Crewe, a pupil of Frank Matcham's who never succeeded in crossing that delicate bridge between brilliance and genius, particularly so far as exterior design and massing is concerned. Faced in terracotta, brick and stone, the three-storey Renaissance façade of the theatre, while elaborate in detail, is essentially two-dimensional, with the insubstantial crowning cupola above the curving entrance bay less than enhanced today by an internally lit modern canopy.

The long, rather narrow, foyer and booking hall, with its pretty ticket office, is restrained in the use of decoration, only to open into an auditorium of spectacular French Renaissance richness. Two tiers of paired bow-fronted boxes, framed by giant Ionic columns, flank a segmental proscenium arch. Above the boxes an arched tympanum contains figure groups displaying personifications of Tragedy, Comedy, Poetry and Music, along with painted roundels depicting rural scenes. The theatrical periodical *The Era* of 23 December 1911 identifies the interior decoration as cream and gold with side panels in autumnal tints. It also draws attention to the domed ceiling, which is sadly now ominously austere

RIGHT Two tiers of paired
boxes between giant
Ionic columns, which
in turn sit on heavy
console brackets,
in a rich French
Renaissance auditorium.

1919 and 1924. George Robey managed the theatre for a short time from 1927, and in 1961 Jack Hilton purchased the freehold. A year later the building was bought by Charles Clore and EMI, who renamed it the Shaftesbury Theatre in 1963. In 1973 the auditorium ceiling collapsed following the successful production of *Hair* (described as a Tribal Love Rock Musical), but the Greater London Council's pressure to have the building listed, together with the efforts of the Save London's Theatres Campaign, turned the tide against demolition. Since the theatre's restoration, successes have included *Jeffrey Bernard is Unwell* with Peter O'Toole (1991) and *Dear Ralph*, starring Ralph Bates, Bernard Cribbins and Sandi Toksvig (1994).

In the entrance foyer a polished timber panel records the formation of the Theatre of Comedy on 8 May 1983, founded by Ray Cooney with members including Wendy Craig, Judi Dench, Maureen Lipman and Geoffrey Palmer. Also on exhibition here is an excellent and informative scale model of the theatre by Brian Gallagher.

ABOVE Detail of column feet flanking bow-fronted box fronts.

ABOVE Diocletian (semicircular) windows alternate with oculi above rather overwhelming advertising panels on the theatre's corner elevation.

in its lack of decoration, but was originally highly ornamented with 'symbolic groups'. The present colour scheme of pale peach and cream, touched with gold, is not unsympathetic to the architecture.

The theatre has seen good times and bad. In 1916 the management was taken over by Seymour Hicks, but it was C. B. Cochran who staged successful productions of Gilbert and Sullivan operas between

SHAKESPEARE'S GLOBE

BANKSIDE

HISTORY

• 1564. William Shakespeare, the third of eight children, born at Stratford-on-Avon, probably on 23 April.

• 1599. First Globe built; burnt down 1613.

• 1614. Globe rebuilt; demolished 1644.

• 1949. Sam Wanamaker makes first visit to London.

• 1970. Globe Playhouse Trust established by Wanamaker.

• 1997. Globe opens on 12 June.

OF SPECIAL INTEREST

• The Globe complex is a tribute to one man's inspired vision as well as an intellectual and constructional exercise. It is also a triumph of planning and design on a constricted site.

• Seating capacity: 1,380, and 500 standing.

ABOVE Detail of the fine plaster- and timberwork on the outer wall of the theatre.

n 2000, as if inspired by an original thought, the government trumpeted the advantages of travelling to the Millennium Dome at Greenwich by river; but at least since the Romans occupied Britain, river traffic has made a major economic contribution to London's prosperity. While in the 16th century London Bridge would afford City residents access to the South Bank, persons of rank and position would arrive at the Globe Theatre by river from Westminster. Only in the decades since the Second World War has the river slowly died, and its industrial waterfront all but disappeared. Where wharves and warehouses stood, a strange leftover world has evolved as governments and local councils have exchanged a unique piece of London's character for a combination of demolition sites, artiness and very lucrative flat and office developments.

Within the Liberty of Holywell (now the London Borough of Hackney), The Theatre, widely supposed to be the first London theatre, was built in 1577, but was short-lived; bedevilled by a disputed lease and structural problems, the building was demolished at the latter end of 1598. Since the medieval period usable structural timbers were rarely discarded: those from The Theatre were transported south of the river to the Liberty of the Clink (now in the London Borough of Southwark) to provide a basic frame for the Globe, which opened in 1599, only to be burnt down and rebuilt in 1613–14. The second Globe was pulled down as a result of Puritan pressure around 1644, and tenement housing was built on the land.

The pinpointing of the theatre site after almost 350 years by Professor John Orrell, and its subsequent excavation by archaeologists from the Museum of London, revealed a fragment of the building beneath Anchor Terrace (1834), a unified yellow stock brick and stucco block of eight houses (now little more than a gutted shell, with entirely modern interiors used as offices) on the east side of the approach to Southwark Bridge. As only a small part of the building could be exposed, little positive information regarding its exact size and even its shape could be established, but an estimated diameter a little in excess of 100 feet places the west wall under the roadway.

For generations the possibility of reconstructing the Globe stimulated much informed discussion, but little more than that – until American actor Sam Wanamaker's first visit to London in 1949. He noted with some surprise and not a little sadness the lack of any theatrical memorial to probably the world's greatest playwright, and some 20 years later, in 1970, he founded the Globe Playhouse Trust, establishing himself as the only individual willing to risk failure in order to achieve his long-term aim.

To build his theatre on the original site was impossible, but some 250 yards to the west, in the lee of Bankside Power Station, now the Tate Modern Gallery, a former council depot on the river front was made available by Southwark Council in 1970, and Wanamaker could at last see a practical way forward. The site, originally occupied by the Anchor Tavern, lies on the western angle of Bankside with New Globe Walk, adjacent to Cardinal's Wharf, a 17th-century house of particular interest, and divided from a pair of brown brick houses (dated 1712) by the extremely narrow Cardinal's Cap Alley. A plaque on the

mas, building contracts and contemporary buildings, is inevitably to court criticism and dispute. Peter McCurdy, whose firm McCurdy and Co. of Stamford Dingley, Berkshire, fabricated the timber work, quite correctly identifies the theatre complex as an educational tool; his quest for accuracy of construction led him through an exercise in meticulous research and analysis involving the detailed study of over 100 buildings of the period, finally producing the details that would be translated into working drawings. Major timbers

ABOVE The golden staircase enclosure to the Globe speaks to us across the centuries.

ABOVE RIGHT The British theatre owes a massive debt to Sam Wanamaker: he believed when others doubted, he pressed forward while others dragged their feet. McCurdy's beautiful timberwork is a fitting memorial from which many will gain knowledge and pleasure.

earlier house records that Sir Christopher Wren lived here during the building of St Paul's Cathedral; this may be no more than legend, although it would have been the ideal place from which to observe the progress of the cathedral work. On the opposite angle of New Globe Walk is a late 20th-century nine-storey block of flats of little interest.

To turn his vision into reality Wanamaker commissioned architect Theo Crosby and sought the collective advice of leading theatre historians. The scheme, if realized, would not only provide for a learned reconstruction of a Shakespearean theatre, it would also present superb educational facilities, a permanent exhibition, a second, smaller theatre based on an early 17th-century example designed by Inigo Jones (architect of the Banqueting Hall in Whitehall) and the extensive support facilities required of a modern complex.

To attempt a three-dimensional reconstruction, based on partial archaeological evidence, panora-

were obtained from all over Great Britain, including some as a gift from the Forestry Commission, taken from the ancient Forest of Dean in Gloucestershire. In fact, McCurdy will tell you that four posts standing together are respectively from England, Scotland, Wales and Northern Ireland. Site work commenced in 1987, and the task of erecting the timber frames began in 1993.

On 12 June 1997 Her Majesty the Queen and His Royal Highness Prince Philip opened the complex, but neither Sam Wanamaker nor Theo Crosby was present to celebrate this massive achievement – for Sam Wanamaker had died on 18 December 1993, and Theo Crosby on 12 September, 1994.

Where many a barge doth saile, and row with are,
Where many a barge doth rest with toppe-royall.
O' towne of townes, patrone and not-compare:
London, though art the floure of cities all.
From 'To the City of London' by William Dunbar, c. 1530

RIGHT View out from the stage, clearly echoing Johannes de Witt's unique drawing of the Swan, taken from the gallery within the tiring house façade.

STRAND THEATRE
ALDWYCH

HISTORY

• 1905. Waldorf Theatre, designed by W. G. R. Sprague for the Waldorf Theatre Syndicate Ltd, opens on 22 May.

• 1909. Name changed to Strand Theatre.

• Statutorily Listed Historic Building: Grade II.

OF SPECIAL INTEREST

• Last three-tier theatre to be built in London.

• The exemplary care given by Sprague to developing his elevational treatment of the theatre.

• The sensitive Louis XIV design of the interior.

• Seating capacity: 1,050.

ABOVE The tympanum above the proscenium arch depicts Apollo reining in his chariot.

RIGHT A putti group holds a wreath above two tiers of semicircular-fronted boxes. The auditorium is handled with panache by Sprague with Hubert van Hooydonk.

OPPOSITE PAGE Elegant in the extreme, the main staircase rises to a semicircular landing and again to the salon above. Stairs either side give access to the stalls bar within an attractive semicircular vestibule.

n the first years of the 20th century the townscape of the West End of London was witnessing immense changes, designed to ease increasing traffic congestion but with the secondary aim of eradicating swaths of undesirable slum dwellings. Amid extensive demolition works, Aldwych was opened in 1905, and among the first buildings to be constructed on this wide, sweeping, crescent roadway were the Strand and Aldwych Theatres, designed by architect W. G. R. Sprague and opened on 22 May and 23 December 1905 respectively. The Strand Theatre, originally the Waldorf, financed by the Waldorf Theatre Syndicate Ltd, is the more southerly, situated on the corner of Catherine Street, while the Aldwych occupies the more northerly angle with Drury Lane. Between the two, and completing the group, is the Waldorf Hotel of 1908 (for more detail, see the Aldwych Theatre, page 22). The theatre's name was changed to the Strand in 1909.

ABOVE Portland stone faced free classical façade. Semicircular headed windows with swagged keystones form a rusticated podium to a great engaged Ionic order. The open-bed pediment is filled with sculpture and swagging.

Shubert was tragically killed in an accident; Lee Shubert took on the management role, but held it only for a matter of months.

Seen from the Aldwych, the theatres are designed as a Portland stone faced free classical reverse pair, completing an almost symmetrical composition with the Waldorf Hotel. However, whereas the flank elevation to the Aldwych Theatre peters out in Drury Lane, the more exposed Strand elevation to Catherine Street continues as a Portland-stone four-storey, 10-bay classical façade divided by giant pilasters above a channelled ground storey.

Internally the theatre is extremely attractive, Sprague here working in partnership with the talented interior decorator Hubert van Hooydonk. The corner entrance vestibule with its 'fruity' ceiling mouldings leads into an elegant Corinthian-pilastered white and gold foyer, incorporating a fine dark, polished timber pay-box front. The cloak-room, opening off the foyer, retains – preserved from modernization by who knows what apparently accidental factors – its attractive green and cream glazed tile decoration, and the beautifully designed main staircase rises to give access to an elliptical dress-circle refreshment saloon of quality, again decorated in white and gold with fluted Corinthian pilasters above a panelled dado.

The lovely three-tier cantilevered auditorium, the last in London to incorporate the third tier, is decorated in a mainly white and gold Louis XIV style. The proscenium, with its stylized lotus flower and acanthus decoration, and its dramatic tympanum depicting Apollo, in his chariot, reining in four fiery horses against a stylized sun, is flanked by stage boxes, themselves emphasized by giant bracketed Ionic pilasters crowned with putti. The dress-circle front is decorated with swags of fruit above a pulvinated bay-leaf band, while the upper-circle and balcony fronts are more simple, utilizing grotesque laughing masks and sunbursts. The domed and painted auditorium ceiling in a heavily moulded surround must once have been striking, but at the time of writing smoke and dirt have obscured, at least for the time being, that undoubted asset.

The theatre opened with *Il Maestro di Capella*, but almost immediately became the temporary home of His Majesty's Theatre company while alterations were made to their building. Over the years the Strand has produced farce and musical comedy, opera and Shakespeare. *A Funny Thing Happened on the Way to the Forum* was a hit here in the mid-1960s, and in the 1970s *No Sex Please – We're British* had a popular extended run.

Aldwych is neither a centre of fashion nor an epicurean paradise; its shops are small and alive with workers from surrounding offices, and some-how it seems to have fallen off the edge of Covent Garden. Opposite the theatre, in Aldwych, is India House (1930), a building of considerable interest designed by Sir Herbert Baker and A. T. Scott, incorporating well-researched decorative motifs and a certain colonial elegance. In Catherine Street, the stone-faced Duchess Theatre overlooks the Strand's long flank elevation. Prior to its completion the Strand was leased to the American Shubert brothers, but only days before the opening Sam

VAUDEVILLE THEATRE
STRAND

HISTORY

• 1869–70. First theatre designed by
C. J. Phipps for William Wybrow Robertson.

• 1890. Front-of-house additions,
again by Phipps.

• 1925–6. Auditorium remodelled by
architect Robert Atkinson for John Maria
and Rocco Gatti.

• Statutorily Listed
Historic Building: Grade II.

OF SPECIAL INTEREST

• The survival of pre-1925 work
in the foyer, auditorium and backstage.

• The retention of stage machinery
and artefacts from the first theatre.

• Seating capacity: 690.

ABOVE Adamesque
plasterwork
decorates the
ceiling of the
foyer.

BELOW
Increasingly rare
timber drum
and shaft
mechanisms,
used to raise and
lower heavy
scenery and
props, are located
above the grid.
Few London
theatres retain
original
machinery, but
the best is to be
found at Her
Majesty's Theatre,
Haymarket and St
Martin's Theatre,
West Street.

n 1869–70 William Robertson, seeing a great deal more profit to be had in theatre building, built the Vaudeville on the site of his failed billiards club. It rose behind two houses, Nos 403 and 404 Strand, to the designs of C. J. Phipps, in a romanesque style. *The Builder* magazine of 23 April 1870 hailed the architect's 'elegant ensemble before the curtain' as 'advantageously lofty', though suggesting with less enthusiasm that arrangements behind the curtain seem 'calculated to lower the character of actors and actresses'.

In 1870 the theatre was leased by Robertson to Thomas Thorne and two others, David James and H. J. Montague. In 1882 Thorne became sole lessee and in 1889 he demolished Nos 403 and 404 Strand to expand his theatre onto the Strand frontage. To carry out this task he engaged C. J. Phipps, who duly provided a new foyer block behind a not unattractive Portland-stone classical façade, four storeys high and five bays wide. Behind the new front he introduced a deceptively large Adamesque foyer, which survives in the present theatre, articulated by pilasters and quite delicate cream and gold decoration, above a polished timber-panelled dado. The staircase giving access to the dress circle is mundane, almost domestic in character. Having carried out the work, Thorne sold the lease of the theatre in 1892 to restaurateurs Agostino and Stefano Gatti, who in 1878 had become lessees of the Adelphi Theatre, only a few doors along the Strand to the west. The buildings around the theatre are poor, doing little to enhance its architecture, but opposite is the grand Shell-Mex House, originally the Cecil Hotel of 1886, designed by Perry and Reed – who also rebuilt the Alhambra Theatre, Leicester Square, in 1883, on a site now occupied by the Odeon.

In 1905 John Maria and Rocco Gatti took over the theatre's management, and in 1925–6 undertook the remodelling of the auditorium, plus the provision of a new dressing-room block extending back to an Adamesque board room, lit by a fine fan-lunetted Venetian window giving onto Maiden Lane. Robert

BELOW Phipps's ceiling of 1870, with Atkinson's remodelled auditorium of 1925–6 below.

RIGHT The restrained Portland-stone, four-storey classical façade under a pitched slate roof.

Atkinson, a pioneer of the super-cinemas of the 1890s, was the architect, and, while retaining the coving and ceiling from the 1890s, he installed a rather stereotyped rectangular Adamesque auditorium, decorated in cream and gold on a blue-grey background.

Behind the proscenium arch the stage is worked from concrete fly floors, utilizing a combination of hemp and counterweighting. A rare early leather thunder drum, about six feet square by one foot deep, and a lightning sheet survive, while above the grid, which is approached by a Jacob's ladder, are two increasingly scarce drum and shaft mechanisms four feet and eight feet in diameter. In the small cellar under the stage two corner traps survive.

The Vaudeville opened on 16 April 1870 with a comedy, *For Love or Money*. Among notable productions since the reconstruction of 1925–6, *Salad Days* was a huge hit in the 1950s, as was *Shirley Valentine* more recently in 1987.

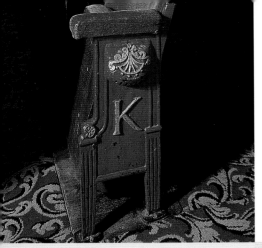

VICTORIA PALACE THEATRE

VICTORIA STREET

HISTORY

• Early 1830s. The Royal Standard Hotel is built in Stockdale Terrace on a site now occupied by Victoria railway station.

• 1886. The Royal Standard rebuilt.

• 1911. Frank Matcham builds the Victoria Palace on the Royal Standard site for Alfred Butt.

• Statutorily Listed Historic Building: Grade II.

OF SPECIAL INTEREST

• The splendid white eye-catching exterior design, carried through to a superb baroque auditorium.

• Seating capacity: 1,575.

ABOVE Searching for your seat, the curtain about to rise, it is hardly the time to study original cast-iron row ends. However, a few moments set aside during the interval are well rewarded.

ictoria Street, completed in the mid-1880s, is a major east–west artery north of the River Thames, linking Victoria Railway Station at its western extremity with the Palace of Westminster and Westminster Bridge to the east. Immediately prior to its construction, the Stag brewery and surrounding areas of slum dwellings stood in sharp contrast with the elegance of Victoria Square and Buckingham Palace, and the forbidding grandeur of the Middlesex House of Correction for Women, all close by. As the new road was put through, slum tenants were rehoused and their hovels demolished, to be rebuilt in a manner rather more acceptable to the residents of Eaton Square and its environs less than half a mile away, bordering on Chelsea.

Prior to the final expansion of Victoria Railway Station in 1905–8, part of its present site was occupied by Stockdale Terrace and the Royal Standard Hotel, built in the early 1830s and licensed for singing and dancing. Owned by John Moy, it was known as Moy's Music Hall before being officially renamed the Royal Standard Concert Rooms. Following major rehabilitation work in 1863, it became the Royal Standard Music Hall, with a two-tier auditorium and an audience capacity approaching 2,500.

In 1886 Richard Wake, its proprietor, rebuilt the Standard on the Victoria Palace site as an enterprise designed to be inviting to the public, combining a high level of audience comfort with restaurant and drinking facilities. By 1910, emphasis in the London theatre was switching markedly towards musical and family-oriented entertainment, a state of affairs not lost on entrepreneur Alfred Butt, who bought the Standard to rebuild it as a variety theatre.

A man of discernment, Butt commissioned architect Frank Matcham to design what turned out to be one of London's theatrical gems – although its immediate setting has been compromised to some degree by a proliferation of

RIGHT The fine safety curtain painted by scenic artist Lisa Dickson (1997) mirrors the auditorium in front of it.

SAFETY CURTAIN

LEFT Overlooking the taxi ranks and bus station that make up the forecourt to Victoria Railway Station is Frank Matcham's scene-stealing front. Built in 1911 by Henry Lovett Ltd, and faced in white glazed faience, the baroque-style theatre is among the prettiest in London.

storeys emphasizes the entrance, while draped female figures flank a central Ionic crowning cupola, topped (until the Blitz) by a sculpture of a pirouetting Pavlova. Removed as a safety precaution during the air raids, the figure is said to have been 'mislaid' – but could it be that she enhances a garden somewhere in the leafy depths of the Home Counties?

A modern canopy shelters two pairs of double doors enriched with flowing glazing bars and bevelled glass, while to the west of the building a single-storey, three-bay wing has now been successfully absorbed into the main theatre foyer to provide additional waiting and ticketing space. Grey marble wall linings with mosaic banding give an air of opulence, without ostentation, to the restrained white and gold Adamesque foyer. At the head of the main staircase rising out of the foyer are fine bronze busts of the Crazy Gang, reviving memories of great shows past.

Matcham was a master of planning and levels, street furniture and an astonishing planning faux pas in the early 1960s that allowed the erection of the gargantuan 334-foot-high Portland House as a totally alien backdrop. With its white glazed faience façade, Matcham's symmetrical baroque building was without doubt designed as an eye-catcher for all who left the railway station. A great central mosaic-lined niche rising through three of the four main

and in a wonderfully rich baroque auditorium of red, gold and cream it would be very easy to miss his slightly unorthodox detail adjustments which click together almost imperceptibly, again demonstrating his genius. The quality of the work extends into the great domed and lunetted ceiling, the lunettes being designed with a gesture in the direction of medieval blind tracery. Even small details, such as the numerous attractive original wall-mounted brass ashtrays, were attended to.

The reeded and ribboned proscenium arch houses an original modern work by scenic artist Lisa Dickson: a safety curtain beautifully painted in 1997 as a fish-eye reflection of the crowded auditorium. Behind the arch, any original timber stage machinery was removed around 1970.

Ever since the days of Alfred Butt the Victoria Palace has been a theatre specializing in variety and musical shows: *Me and My Girl* played over 1,000 performances from 16 December 1938, and for 15 years from 1947 the Crazy Gang took the stage; they were followed by *The Black and White Minstrel Show*, which ran for 10 years until 1972. More recent productions have included *The Pyjama Game* with Lesley Ash and Anita Dobson (1999) and *The Rocky Horror Show*, starring Jason Donovan (also 1999), while *Annie* (1998) and *Buddy* (1989–95) have also filled the theatre.

WESTMINSTER THEATRE
PALACE STREET

alace Street exhibits a welcome variety of textures and styles, apart from the intrusive 27 storeys of Stag Place and 16 Palace Street – buildings that supplanted the Stag brewery in 1959, thus ending its 500-year history in Westminster. Late 19th-century buildings harmonize with well-mannered houses of the 18th century in Buckingham Place and Catherine Place, and at its northern end the Westminster Theatre occupies a prime site where the road kinks slightly, a deviation dictated by the presence of an earlier building at this point. Opposite the theatre a plaque fixed to Stafford Mansions records: 'The Free French Naval Forces H.Q. were harboured in this house by the British People 1940–45.'

The earlier building on the site was the Charlotte Chapel, a preaching box built by William Dodd, chaplain to George III, in 1766 as a chapel-of-ease to St Peter's, Eaton Square; indeed, by the late 19th century it was also known as St Peter's Chapel. In 1921 the chapel was deconsecrated, and, with extensive alterations by J. Stanley Beard (a talented architect who also designed three particularly fine Forum cinemas in London for Herbert A. Yapp), it was reopened in 1923 as the St James's Picture Theatre. The building closed again in 1931, when A. B. Horne, who also went under the name of Anmer Hall, bought it and with designers Arnold Dunbar Smith and Molly MacArthur converted it to theatre use, opening as the Westminster Theatre on 7 October 1931 with James Bridie's *The Anatomist*.

In 1938 the London Mask Theatre was established in the building by J. B. Priestley and Ronald Jeans, with a permanent company including Michael Denison, and in March 1939 the first performance of T. S. Eliot's *The Family Reunion* was given here. On Remembrance Day 1946 the theatre was commissioned to pay homage to the men and women of the evangelistic Moral Rearmament movement, founded by the American Frank Buchanan, who fell in the Second World War. Moral Rearmament took over the Westminster Theatre in the early 1960s and until 1966 used it to put on its own moralistic plays and films, most of them written by Peter Howard. The theatre has remained unlicensed since its Moral Rearmament days, though somewhat ironically, immediately outside the main entrance is the Phoenix pub, built in the 1930s on the site of an earlier drinking house.

The theatre's vertical slate exterior cladding, associated with a rebuilding project of the mid-1960s by John and Sylvia Reid, gives the building a rather fashionable but gloomy appearance, which is not relieved in the low-ceilinged foyer/refreshment area; the single-tier auditorium retained from the 1930s conversion comes in consequence as an uplifting revelation. Pink, red and gold colourings, with palmette and griffin panels, provide an unlikely combination of space and intimacy.

The Anatomist was again produced at the theatre in 1948, starring Alastair Sim and George Cole, and it was here that Flora Robson starred in *Black Chiffon* in 1949. *Annie* was produced here in 1967, and in 1978 Paul Jones starred in *Joseph and the Amazing Technicolour Dreamcoat*. In 1987 the theatre staged *An Inspector Calls* with Tom Baker and in 1988 *The Miracle Worker* starring Daryl Black.

ABOVE LEFT The shadowy pianist provides an intimate moment in this 1930s auditorium.

ABOVE Front elevation of the mid-1960s by architects John and Sylvia Reid.

WHITEHALL THEATRE
WHITEHALL

HISTORY

• 1929–30. Designed by Edward A. Stone in collaboration with Marc Henri and Gaston Laverdet for Walter Hackett.

• 1930. Theatre opens on 29 September.

• Statutorily Listed Building: Grade II.

ABOVE Decoration by Marc Henri and Gaston Laverdet, 1929–30.

OF SPECIAL INTEREST

• The Art Deco interior.

• Seating capacity: 648.

he theatre lies on the west side of Whitehall, just where the roadway narrows to enter Trafalgar Square, to the north of the extended ranges of government buildings. Built on a vacant site left after the demolition of the Old Ship Tavern, a 17th-century inn, the theatre extends back to Spring Gardens, the site of famous 17th-century pleasure grounds, immortalized by Sir John Vanbrugh in his play *The Provok'd Wife*. Here also stood the concert hall where Mozart made his London debut in 1764.

Designed by Edward A. Stone in 1929–30, the building is fabricated in steel and reinforced concrete with the front and rear elevations faced in Portland stone. The front elevation, with its wide, triple-arched centre bay and narrow wings, is clean in a modernistic mode, quite out of step with its immediate surroundings. Adjacent on its north side is a fine bank building of 1885 by George Aitchison, while opposite the theatre is an array of excellent buildings including the Old Shades pub (1898), designed in a free Flemish-Gothic style by Treadwell and Martin, and Craigs Court, laid out in 1695; its surviving mansion, originally backing onto the grounds of Northumberland House, was demolished in 1874 to make space for Northumberland Avenue.

Although Stone designed the envelope of the Whitehall, the interiors are the work of Marc Henri and Gaston Laverdet, who collaborated with Stone at the Piccadilly Theatre (1928) and the Prince Edward Theatre (1930). At this peak

RIGHT The theatre's Portland-stone, Art Deco façade to Whitehall.

ABOVE The single-balcony auditorium is enlivened by economical but effective Art Deco forms in a richly coloured space.

of theatre-building activity in London, they had also, with Ewen S. Barr, designed the Duchess Theatre in Catherine Street (1929).

Under a modern canopy three pairs of armour-glass doors give access to a satinwood-lined rectangular foyer which also serves as the circle bar. A glazed screen then opens into the intimate auditorium, where the surface decoration can only be described as economical. The tympanum to the ribbed and angled proscenium arch contains a stylized mermaid emerging from a shell, and the overall geometry of this Germanic 'architecture of light' creation combines with a subtle scheme of concealed lighting to create a remarkable effect in this single-balcony, silver, red, gold and black space. The rectangular stalls bar, which continues the theme of the auditorium, is said to be based on a liner's saloon, a reference to the romance of ocean

travel in the 1930s. Restored with great care in 1985 by Ian Albury, the building serves as an object lesson in fabric conservation to owners of any British theatre.

Built by Walter Hackett for the staging of light comedy, the theatre has in fact been through a number of changes. In the early 1940s striptease queen Phyllis Dixey featured in a series of saucy shows, followed by a run of farces. The 1950s and 1960s saw Brian Rix present wonderfully successful productions, including *Dry Rot* (1954) and *Simple Spymen* (1958). In 1961 Paul Raymond, better known for his Revue Bar, brought in the daring *Pyjama Tops*, starring Caroline Dudley, before unsuccessfully attempting to convert the theatre into a tourist-oriented War Museum. In the hands of the Ambassadors Theatre Group the building has now been restored to its proper use.

WINDMILL THEATRE
GREAT WINDMILL STREET

n the 18th century a windmill stood at the head of the rising ground that is now Great Windmill Street, but intense development of the semi-rural landscape made it redundant. Since that time the area has continued to evolve, and later buildings have superseded the original expansion.

It would be very easy to walk past the theatre without noticing it. Situated adjacent to the stage door of the Lyric Theatre, Shaftesbury Avenue, it was erected in 1897 as part of Piccadilly Buildings. Licensed as a cinema in 1910 to accommodate about 350 people, its capacity was later almost doubled by the addition of a balcony. Following an extensive remodelling by architect Howard Jones in 1930 the building opened as a theatre. At that time it was faced in glazed white terracotta, and designed in a French style with two added pepper-pot towers; the black sheet cladding probably dates from the 1980s.

During the 1940s and 1950s the Windmill was one of the most famous theatres in Britain. In the early 1930s the building's owner, Mrs Laura Henderson, with Vivian van Damm, had decided to introduce non-stop revue, achieving spectacular effects within a very small space under the title *Revudeville*. After a slow start, a winning combination of young comedians, including Tony Hancock and Jimmy Edwards, with beautiful static nude tableaux, drew enthusiastic audiences throughout the Second World War and beyond, until 1964, when it converted to casino/cinema use. Closed for only a fortnight in September 1939, the theatre stayed in business for the remainder of the war, earning it (just about) the right to say, 'We Never Closed.' In 1976 the building was adapted to house a theatre/restaurant, and live entertainment has continued, in one form or another, since that date.

ABOVE A window detail from the 1930s' remodelling.

RIGHT General exterior view from the south. On the extreme right is part of Dr William Hunter's house, which has been absorbed into the backstage of the Lyric Theatre.

WYNDHAM'S THEATRE
CHARING CROSS ROAD

HISTORY

• 1899. Designed by W. G. R. Sprague for (Sir) Charles Wyndham and Mary Moore, and built on the Marquess of Salisbury's estate.

• Statutorily Listed Historic Building: Grade II*.

OF SPECIAL INTEREST

• A perfect example of how judicious planning can achieve an illusion of space on a very restricted site.

• One of the finest theatre interiors in London.

• Totally hemp-worked fly-floors, now a rare survival.

• Seating capacity: 750.

ABOVE Allegorical winged figures surround framed portraits of Goldsmith and Sheridan above the richly decorated proscenium. It is thought that the central bust could have been modelled to represent Mary Moore.

RIGHT The part elevation to Charing Cross Road is a Portland-stone free-classic essay of fine quality.

yndham's Theatre is situated on the western edge of Covent Garden, close to the junction of Charing Cross Road with Cranbourne Street, amid a mass of street furniture. The building occupies an island site, which prior to their demolition in 1897 supported some dozen small units, including a pub. It is divided from its neighbours by St Martin's Court, a narrow pedestrian way paved with York stone, which precludes any possible expansion beyond its existing yellow stock-brick outer walls. To its north a dull stone block of the 1930s gives access to Leicester Square underground station, and a plaque records the birth here in 1859 of Sidney Webb, the Fabian socialist and gradualist social reformer. In an area once famous for 'horsy and fighting men', the neighbouring Round Table pub is said to have housed American John C. Heenan before his championship fight with Englishman Tom Sayers at the end of the 18th century.

Sir Charles Wyndham was born in Liverpool in 1837 and christened Charles Culverwell. The son of a surgeon, he studied medicine in London and Dublin, qualifying in 1858, but at the same time and – against his father's wishes – he harboured a burning desire to become an actor. In 1862 Culverwell joined the federal army to serve as a surgeon in the American Civil War, taking leave from his duties during the winter months to appear on the New York stage. In 1865 he returned home to pursue a theatrical career, changing his name to Wyndham along the way. In 1875 he became actor–manager at the Criterion Theatre, and it was here that he met the 23-year-old actress Mary Moore, already married to playwright James Albery (who died of cirrhosis of the liver in 1889) and a mother of three children. Beautiful and clever, Mary became Wyndham's leading lady and business partner, and his wife only three years before his death in 1919. By that time they owned three West End theatres, the Criterion, Wyndham's and the New (now the Albery Theatre) in St Martin's Lane; and Charles Wyndham had become Sir Charles, having been knighted for services to the

RIGHT A particularly pretty circular foyer decorated with a lightness of touch by W. G. R. Sprague. The prominent semicircular ticket deck is modern, and the original ticket-office doors survive either side of the theatre entrance.

ABOVE This beautiful, little-altered Louis XVI auditorium features three tiers of ornate bow-fronted boxes, the upper (grand circle) being decorated with lion-head masks and medallions.

the Marquess of Salisbury, upon whose land the buildings stood, so admired Wyndham as an actor that this opposition was summarily despatched, and the site was Wyndham's – provided he could raise the purchase price and subsequent building costs. He was not a wealthy man, and it was Mary Moore who rescued a potentially difficult situation, raising the money through her society connections.

To design his theatre, Charles Wyndham commissioned the 34-year-old W. G. R. Sprague, an admirer of the French and Italian Renaissance. In Wyndham's – one of eight theatres that Sprague had on his drawing board in 1899 – he produced the epitome of European civic theatre architecture overlaid with an English sense of good breeding and quiet confidence. Faced in Portland stone, the free classical façade of two and three storeys is three major bays wide. The central bay has a balustrade loggia at first-floor level, and a crowning pediment containing a bust of Shakespeare flanked by muses and cherubs. The foyer entrance is to the left of the façade, leading through enriched doors to a very pretty circular blue and gold foyer with a small but attractive staircase, which, in turn, gives way to one of London's most beautiful and little-altered auditoria. Elegant and sophisticated, it is decorated in a Louis XVI style, retaining the original turquoise blue and cream colour scheme described in *The Era* of November 1899, with painted panels of flowers and leaves on the royal-circle front, and lion-head masks and medallions, in painted panel, on the grand-circle front. The steeply raked balcony rises up from the rear of the grand circle. The richly gilded architectural proscenium is dominated by three-dimensional allegorical figures and flanked by three tiers of bow-fronted boxes between Corinthian pilasters. The circular ceiling comprises four very fine painted panels after François Boucher, an 18th-century painter of pastorals.

Although little survives of the original timber sub-stage machinery, the fly-floors, miraculously, are fully hemp-worked. While this is a rare and rewarding sight, it is, at the same time, easy to appreciate why at the Theatre Royal, Leicester, in 1865 it was recommended that a small fire engine should be kept in the flys.

The theatre opened with David Garrick in a play by T. W. Robertson, and has since staged many successes, including J. M. Barrie's *Dear Brutus* (1917), Edgar Wallace's *The Ringer* (1926) and, after the Second World War, *Quiet Weekend*, which ran for 1,059 performances. More recent successes include *The Prime of Miss Jean Brodie* (1966) *Godspell* (1972) and *Art* (now showing).

theatre in 1902, an accolade that ensured his acceptance into the polite society of Edwardian England.

Having found success on the London stage by the late 1890s, Wyndham turned to pursue his longstanding ambition to establish his own theatre. The buildings on the Charing Cross Road site were in a state of decay, and ripe for redevelopment. A Mr Pyke had also noted the island's potential, but

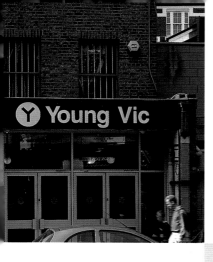

YOUNG VIC THEATRE
THE CUT

Some 150 yards to the west of the Old Vic, in an area of London that is now 'up and coming', is the Young Vic, which was founded by Frank Dunlop under the wing of the National Theatre in 1970. The architectural practice of Howell, Killick, Partridge and Amis – on the face of it an unusual choice, associated as it was with London County Council housing and various Cambridge colleges – was commissioned to design this rather unconventional theatre for young adults; and, mainly from the drawing board of William Gough Howell, there emerged an inspired low-budget solution.

A bombsite facing Short Street and terraces of red-brick shops and flats of about 1900 was selected as the location, and it was decided to retain one three-storey 19th-century house, with its bungalow shop, within the site. Thus Wilson Bros, 66 The Cut, became the main entrance foyer to the complex, with its attractive green and white patterned wall tiling. To the right of No. 66 the chamfered auditorium block was added, providing a 24-foot-high flexible space for dance or conventional drama, and to the left a studio with café, all contained within a raw concrete-block shell. Access to storage and workshops is from the rear in Cons Street.

Dame Sybil Thorndike opened the theatre on 11 December 1970, with Frank Dunlop directing an adaptation of Molière's *The Cheats of Scapino*. Since that time a wide variety of plays have been successfully performed, including *The Taming of the Shrew*, *Waiting For Godot*, *Rosencrantz and Guildenstern are Dead* and *French Without Tears*. The theatre is now independent, with its own board of management.

ABOVE Wilson Bros shop at 66 The Cut survived to become the main entrance to the theatre.

RIGHT Rehearsals in the main auditorium – an unadorned space that leaves unobscured the electrical fittings that are often so essential to productions.

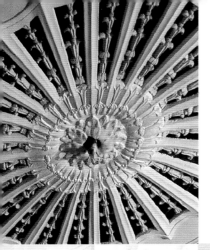

CARLTON THEATRE
HAYMARKET

Following the Fortune Theatre, the Carlton was the second new theatre to be opened in London after the end of the First World War. Situated on the west side of Haymarket, this fine building was designed in an Italianate style by Frank T. Verity and his son-in-law Samuel Beverley in 1926 for the Carlton Theatre company. It opened on 27 April 1927, combining dual theatre and cinema use. The stone-faced façade of five central bays is flanked by narrow set-back single-window wide pavilions. Conceived with a deft lightness of touch, but now swamped by cinema hoardings and a new canopy, the theatre was sold to Paramount and in May 1929 became a permanent cinema.

An attractive Adamesque foyer extends across the front of the building, giving access at street level to the royal and upper circles, within a superbly detailed and proportioned auditorium. In 1954, Twentieth Century Fox took over the cinema, and in 1969 put together a scheme to incorporate three screens within one cinema which failed to materialize. After a second failed subdivision proposal in 1977 the cinema closed, and it was hoped by many that the building would revert to its original theatre use. Cinema historian David Atwell and the Historic Buildings Division of the Greater London Council fought a hard campaign to have the building listed, but the government, under pressure from property interests, brushed the proposal aside. The stage area was subsequently redeveloped as offices and the theatre, now owned by Classic, was split into three screens, opening in January 1979; and so it remains.

The fate of the Carlton Theatre clearly illustrates that vigilance is required at all times to ensure the future of London's irreplaceable theatre buildings, whose delicate fabrics occupy potential sites for very lucrative developments.

ABOVE The pretty Adamesque foyer, extending across the front of the building, is all that remains intact of a theatre building of the highest quality. The government's failure by 1979 to add the theatre to the Statutory List of Buildings of Special Architectural Interest ensured its demise.

ABOVE LEFT Detail of the fanned ceiling centrepiece.

LONDON HIPPODROME
CRANBOURNE STREET

HISTORY

• 1900. Designed by architect
Frank Matcham for (Sir)
Edward Moss.

• 1957. Converted to
theatre/restaurant.

• 2001. In current use as
high-tech entertainment/
presentation venue.

• Statutorily Listed
Historic Building: Grade II.

OF SPECIAL INTEREST

• Surviving remains of
Matcham's theatre.

As the name implies, the London Hippodrome (built by Sir Edward Moss of the Moss Empires Group) started life, on 15 January 1900, as a circus and water spectacular. Today the theatre building, shops and chambers – Cranborne Mansions and the now defunct Crown public house – occupy a prominent five-storey island block above an entrance to Leicester Square underground station, at the junction of Cranbourne Street with Charing Cross Road. To walk round this block today is to experience three totally contrasting aspects of London's character. Along Little Newport Street are the oriental shops on the southern edge of Chinatown; there are the dusty bookshops of Charing Cross Road; while pedestrianized Cranbourne Street offers bargain theatre tickets and fast food to the capital's young.

Not only were the early productions spectacular, but the circus arena and the stage could be hydraulically raised and lowered to provide a 100,000 gallon water tank, filled from an underground river, for aquatic animal acts and scenic creations. By 1909 the circus had run its course, the arena was replaced by stalls seating, and this flexible theatre became variety oriented until August 1957, when it closed for conversion to The Talk of the Town, a theatre–restaurant. Today, the building houses a multi-use high-tech venue offering a wide range of entertainment and presentation facilities.

Designed by architect Frank Matcham for Edward Moss in free French Renaissance style, with a quite dramatic baroque skyline of rearing chariot horses above an open ironwork dome, the building is faced in red sandstone, with caryatid decoration to first-floor windows. Inside, little survives of the superb Matcham theatre below the original upper circle and gods, apart from fragmentary remains of the water tank. It is only at the top, among a conglomeration of high-level metal walkways and electrical paraphernalia, that the ghosts of Lupino Lane, Seymour Hicks, George Robey and Arthur Askey can be felt – if not heard – in the unsettling quiet. Here, where the stepped seating stretches back into the darkness,

ABOVE AND ABOVE LEFT Little remains of Frank Matcham's Hippodrome Theatre, but this remnant from the upper circle and gods – lost in darkness and almost enmeshed in modern metalwork – has seen and heard some of Britain's greatest performers.

above the modern chromium and glass, are free-standing Ionic columns and balustrading, the ghostly imprint of the proscenium arch decoration on the basic plain brickwork and skeletal fly-floors above the stage. A true piece of theatrical archaeology.

LONDON PAVILION
PICCADILLY CIRCUS

The dramatic demolition works required to create Shaftesbury Avenue, which opened in 1886, removed the music hall of Loibl and Sonhammer; this had been established in 1859 on the site of the Black Horse stable yard, leaving an adequate but slightly awkward triangular plot, backing onto Great Windmill Street, upon which to build a new theatre – the second on the site.

The site was rented from the Metropolitan Board of Works by Robert E. Villiers, and the architects commissioned to undertake the scheme were James Saunders and Robert Worley: Worley would design the envelope of the building and the integral Piccadilly Restaurant, while Saunders handled all other aspects. Site operations started in May 1885. The auditorium, designed by J. M. Boekbinder in a Louis XV style, would run parallel to Great Windmill Street, with the main entrance to the theatre from Piccadilly Circus. The restaurant fitted neatly into the western angle of the building. The interior was remodelled by architects Wylson and Long in 1900 and again by an unknown architect in 1918.

The three elevations are symmetrical compositions in an eclectic classical style, the whole being faced in Portland and Bath stone, now painted a yellowy cream. It must have seemed that with its tetrastyle giant Corinthian column portico the building could not fail to make a resounding statement, and yet it has never dominated the Circus.

The theatre first opened in 1885; presenting variety and music-hall programmes, it thrived up to the 1920s. After a short season of film in the late 1920s and early 1930s, the theatre boxes were removed and the proscenium arch enlarged to provide a permanent cinema. For many years the building's main elevations were almost totally obscured by illuminated advertising, which was finally removed in the 1980s. Now gutted, the building houses Madame Tussaud's Rock Circus, with a bland throughway access at cellar level from Piccadilly Circus underground station to London Trocadero – a popular, colourful shopping mall incorporating 'Funland'. Here, in the skeletal remains of the theatre, is a poignant reminder of the potential fragility of London's theatres.

ABOVE LEFT A draped female figure stands poised on the skyline.

ABOVE The part elevation to Coventry Street of Robert Worley's Pavilion scheme.

SAVILLE THEATRE
SHAFTESBURY AVENUE

HISTORY

• 1931. Designed by architects T. P. Bennett and Son with Bertie Crewe, the theatre opens on 8 October.

• 1970. Theatre closes; converted to offices and twin cinemas.

• Statutorily Listed Historic Building: Grade II.

OF SPECIAL INTEREST

• Sculptured stone frieze and five roundels by Gilbert Bayes on the front elevation.

The northern stretch of Shaftesbury Avenue, originally Dudley Street, between Charing Cross Road and St Giles High Street, perpetuates the line of the boundary wall to St Giles Hospital, which was closed by Henry VIII at the dissolution of the monasteries in 1539. Removed from the theatreland atmosphere of the Avenue's southern arm as it curves down into Piccadilly Circus, the buildings are, for the most part, fairly commonplace, apart from one outstanding block on the west side – which includes the Saville.

The Saville Theatre, which opened on 8 October 1931 with a performance of *For the Love of Mike*, was designed by T. P. Bennett and Son with Bertie Crewe for impresario A. E. Fournier. The practice went on to design London Odeon cinemas at Haverstock Hill (mid-1930s, with its opulent gold coloured interior), Highgate (1955, demolished 1974) and Marble Arch (1966).

The steel-framed building of the Saville is an extremely fine composition reminiscent of the Odeon on Shepherd's Bush Green by Frank T. Verity (1923), with its giant arched asymmetrical entrance. Clad in finely laid channelled brown brickwork above a rusticated stone plinth, the building avoids austerity by the introduction of a full-width stone frieze by Gilbert Bayes, who also sculpted the *Queen of Time* statue on Selfridge's store in Oxford Street. *Drama Through The Ages* is a superb and strangely unsung work of art, and as a bonus, the architects also designed into the elevation five high-level roundel plaques by the same artist.

The theatre closed in 1970 and was converted partly to offices and partly into twin cinemas built into a completely remodelled auditorium.

In the late 1950s Stanley Baxter and Evelyn Laye played here in *The Amorous Prawn*, and the lovely Millicent Martin starred in *The Lord Chamberlain Regrets…!* before finding fame in television.

ABOVE LEFT An unsung work of art, Bayes' frieze contains many characters from the world of theatre, such as this enigmatic jester.

ABOVE Gilbert Bayes' stone frieze, *Drama Through the Ages* (1931) is beautifully carved and sited on the building at a height where it can be appreciated.

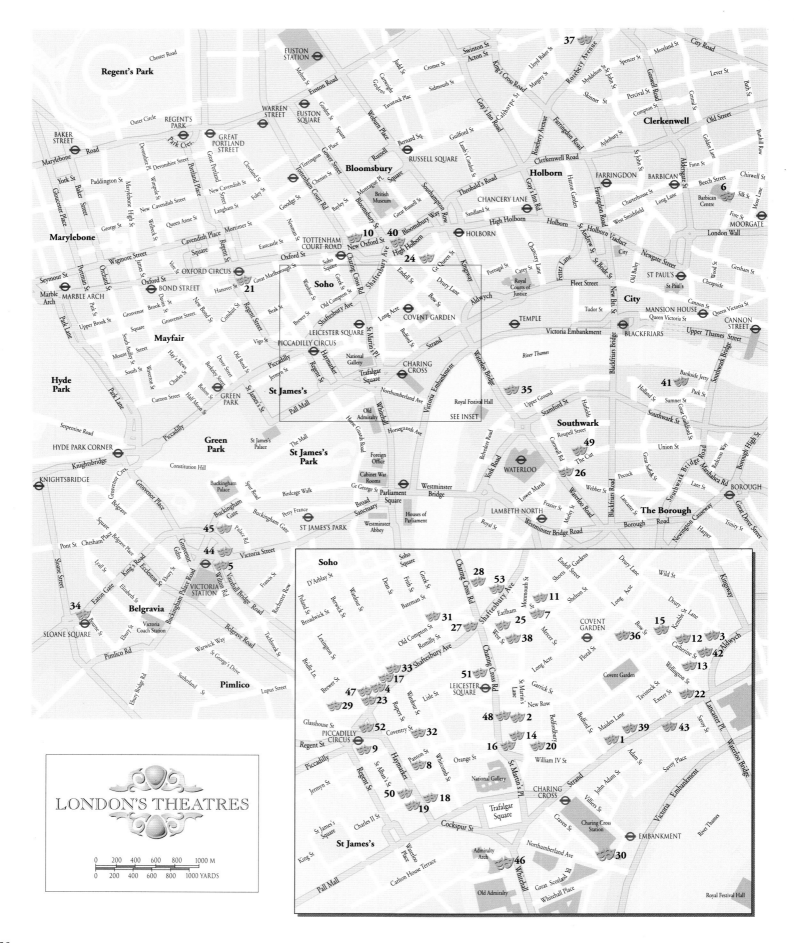

LONDON'S THEATRES

0 200 400 600 800 1000 M

0 200 400 600 800 1000 YARDS

LOCATIONS AND ADDRESSES

1 ADELPHI THEATRE: Strand, WC2E 7NA. Box Office: 020 7344 0055.

2 ALBERY THEATRE: St Martin's Lane, WC2N 4AH. Box Office: 020 7369 1740. Website: www.theambassadors.com

3 ALDWYCH THEATRE: Aldwych, WC2B 4DF. Box Office: 0870 400 0805. Website: www.aldwychtheatre.com

4 APOLLO THEATRE: 29 Shaftesbury Avenue, W1V 7HD. Box Office: 020 7494 5399. Website: www.stoll-moss.com

5 APOLLO VICTORIA THEATRE: 17 Wilton Road, SW1V 1LL. Box Office: 0870 400 0651.

6 BARBICAN THEATRE: Silk Street, EC2Y 8DS. Box Office: 020 7638 8891. Website: www.barbican.org.uk

7 CAMBRIDGE THEATRE: Earlham Street, Seven Dials, WC2 9HU. Box Office: 020 7494 5399. Website: www.stoll-moss.com

8 COMEDY THEATRE: Panton Street, SW1 4DN. Box Office: 020 7369 1731. Website: www.theambassadors.com

9 CRITERION THEATRE: Piccadilly Circus, W1V 9LB. Box Office: 020 7413 1437.

10 DOMINION THEATRE: Tottenham Court Road, W1P 0AG. Box Office: 0870 606 3400.

11 DONMAR WAREHOUSE: 41 Earlham Street, WC2H 9LD. Box Office: 020 7369 1732. Websites: www. donmar-warehouse.com, www.theambassadors.com

12 DRURY LANE – THEATRE ROYAL: Catherine Street, WC2B 5JF. Box Office: 020 7494 5399. Website: www.stoll-moss.com

13 DUCHESS THEATRE: Catherine Street, WC2B 5LA. Box Office: 020 7494 5399. Website: www.stoll-moss.com

14 DUKE OF YORK'S THEATRE: St Martin's Lane, WC2N 4BG. Box Office: 020 7369 1791. Website: www.theambassadors.com

15 FORTUNE THEATRE: Russell Street, WC2B 5HH. Box Office: 020 7836 2238.

16 GARRICK THEATRE: Charing Cross Road, WC2H 0HH. Box Office: 020 7494 5399. Website: www.stoll-moss.com

17 GIELGUD THEATRE: Shaftesbury Avenue, W1V 8AR. Box Office: 020 7494 5399. Website: www.stoll-moss.com

18 HAYMARKET – THEATRE ROYAL: Haymarket, SW1Y 4HT. Box Office: 0870 901 3356. Website: www.trh.co.uk

19 HER MAJESTY'S THEATRE: Haymarket, SW1Y 4QR. Box Office: 020 7494 5399. Website: www.stoll-moss.com

20 LONDON COLISEUM: St Martin's Lane, WC2N 4ES. Box Office: 020 7632 8300. Website: www.eno.org

21 LONDON PALLADIUM: Argyll Street, W1V 1AD. Box Office: 020 7494 5399. Website: www.stoll-moss.com

22 LYCEUM THEATRE: Wellington Street, WC2E 7DA. Box Office: 0870 243 9000.

23 LYRIC THEATRE: Shaftesbury Avenue, W1V 7HA. Box Office: 020 7494 5399. Website: www.stoll-moss.com

24 NEW LONDON THEATRE: Drury Lane, WC2B 5PW. Box Office: 020 7494 5399. Website: www.stoll-moss.com

25 NEW AMBASSADORS THEATRE: West Street, WC2H 9ND. Box Office: 020 7369 1761. Website: www.theambassadors.com

26 OLD VIC THEATRE: Waterloo Road, SE1 8NB. Box Office: 020 7369 1762.

27 PALACE THEATRE: Cambridge Circus, Shaftesbury Avenue, W1D 5AY. Box Office: 020 7494 5399. Website: www.stoll-moss.com

28 PHOENIX THEATRE: Charing Cross Road, WC2H 0JP. Box Office: 020 7369 1733. Website: www.theambassadors.com

29 PICCADILLY THEATRE: Denman Street, W1V 8DY. Box Office: 020 7369 1744. Website: www.theambassadors.com

30 PLAYHOUSE THEATRE: Northumberland Avenue, WC2N 5DN. Box Office: 020 7839 4401

31 PRINCE EDWARD THEATRE: 30 Old Compton Street, W1D 4HS. Box Office: 020 7447 5400. Website: www.delfont-mackintosh.com

32 PRINCE OF WALES THEATRE: 31 Coventry Street, W1D 6AS. Box Office: 020 7839 5972/5987. Website: www.delfont-mackintosh.com

33 QUEEN'S THEATRE: Shaftesbury Avenue, W1V 7HA. Box Office: 020 7494 5399. Website: www.stoll-moss.com

34 ROYAL COURT THEATRE: Sloane Square, SW1W 8AS. Box Office: 020 7565 5000. Website: www.royalcourttheatre.com

35 ROYAL NATIONAL THEATRE: South Bank, SE1 9PX. Box Office: 020 7452 3000. Website: www.nationaltheatre.org.uk

36 ROYAL OPERA HOUSE: Covent Garden, WC2E 9DD. Box Office: 020 7304 4000/ 020 7212 9460. Website: www.royalopera.org

37 SADLER'S WELLS: Rosebery Avenue, EC1R 4TN. Box Office: 020 7863 8000. Website: www.sadlers-wells.com

38 ST MARTIN'S THEATRE: West Street, WC2H 8DP. Box Office: 020 7836 1443.

39 SAVOY THEATRE: Strand, WC2R 0ET. Box Office: 020 7836 8888. Website: www.savoy-group.co.uk

40 SHAFTESBURY THEATRE: 210 Shaftesbury Avenue, WC2H 8DP. Box Office: 0870 906 3798.

41 SHAKESPEARE'S GLOBE: New Globe Walk, Southwark, SE1 9DT. Box Office: 020 7401 9919. Website: www.shakespeares-globe.org

42 STRAND THEATRE: The Aldwych, WC2B 4LD. Box Office: 0870 901 3356. Website: www.trh.co.uk

43 VAUDEVILLE THEATRE: Strand, WC2R 0NH. Box Office: 020 7836 9987.

44 VICTORIA PALACE THEATRE: Victoria Street, SW1E 5EA. Box Office: 020 7834 1317.

45 WESTMINSTER THEATRE: 12 Palace Street, SW1E 5JF. Box Office: 020 7834 0283.

46 WHITEHALL THEATRE: Whitehall, SW1A 2DY. Box Office: 020 7369 1735. Website: www.theambassadors.com

47 WINDMILL THEATRE: 17–19 Great Windmill Street, W1D 7JZ. Box Office: 020 7439 3558.

48 WYNDHAM'S THEATRE: Charing Cross Road, WC2H 0DA. Box Office: 020 7369 1736. Website: www.theambassadors.com

49 YOUNG VIC THEATRE: 66 The Cut, Waterloo, SE1 8LZ. Box Office: 020 7928 6363. Website: www.youngvic.org

50 CARLTON HAYMARKET: 63–65 Haymarket, SW1Y 4RQ. Box Office: 0870 907 0712.

51 HIPPODROME: 1 Cranbourn Street, WC2H 7JH

52 LONDON PAVILION: Piccadilly Circus, W1

53 SAVILLE: Shaftesbury Avenue, WC2

GLOSSARY

ACANTHUS   Genus of perennial plant, whose classical formalized leaf is employed as enrichment and as a characteristic of the Corinthian and Composite capitals.

ACT-DROP   A painted curtain dropped in at the end of each act.

ADAMESQUE   Relating to or derived from the architecture of Scots brothers Robert (1728–92) and James (1732–94) Adam, whose works included alterations to Drury Lane Theatre and Syon House, Middlesex.

ANTHEMION   Honeysuckle and palm leaf pattern common in Greek and Roman architectural decoration.

APRON   Extension of the stage floor beyond the proscenium into the auditorium.

'ASPHALEIA' SYSTEM   Developed as a reaction to the 'Ring' Theatre fire in Vienna, 1881, in which 450 people died, the theory being that if the stage area is constructed in metals then the risks are substantially reduced.

ARABESQUE   Fanciful surface ornament adopted by Renaissance artists, derived from intertwined tendrils and flowers in a symmetrical pattern.

ARCHITRAVE   Formalized beam or lintel forming the lower part of an entablature.

ART DECO   European and American style evolving in the 1920s and 1930s to embrace strongly coloured Ancient Egyptian and Aztec based forms.

ART NOUVEAU   Relatively short-lived European style, prevalent from the 1880s until the First World War, based on undulating asymmetrical curves and plant forms.

ASHLAR   Finely dressed stone wall facings laid in courses with thin joints.

BAROQUE   A theatrically enthusiastic reaction to standardized classical forms, involving dramatic, elaborate modelling and illusion. Popular in England between c.1675 and 1720.

BEAUX ARTS   Ornate classical style emanating from the Ecole Nationale Supérieure des Beaux-Arts, popular from c. 1850 to 1914.

BOMBÉ   Convex.

BRIDGE   Substantial open timber frame forming part of stage floor, raised and lowered by hand, electrical or hydraulic power.

BUCRANIUM   Ox-head or ox-skull ornament, often hung with garlands.

BUSH-HAMMER   A mechanical hammer with a grooved head which produces a rough-finished concrete surface.

CANTILEVER   Member – beam, step, etc. – projecting from vertical wall face and fixed by a dead load at one end.

CAPITAL   Decorative head of a column or pilaster.

CARTOUCHE   Classical tablet in an elaborate ornamental frame, common in baroque decoration from the 17th century.

CHAMFER   The meeting of two perpendicular surfaces, cut off symmetrically at 45°. An asymmetrical cut-off is referred to as a splay.

CHANNELLING   Grooved channels emphasizing the strength of the facework, running horizontally and vertically, highlighting each individual stone.

CHERUB   Plump, angelic, winged male child; contrast with putto, the fat wingless child.

CHEVRON   Device of V-shape or zigzag pattern common in romanesque architecture.

COFFER   Sunken panels in ceilings, domes or vaults, normally square or polygonal.

COLONNADE   Columns formed in a straight line supporting an entablature.

COPING   Brick, stone or concrete wall-top protection.

CORINTHIAN   Third order of Greek architecture; see also Doric, Ionic.

CORNER TRAP   Single traps, usually either side of the downstage grave trap, to project an actor rapidly onto the stage. Also known as bristle traps, demon traps and, more familiarly, star traps.

CORNICE   In classical or Renaissance architecture, the topmost section of an entablature.

COUNTERWEIGHTING   A labour-saving system over traditional hemp-working whereby iron or lead weights are used in cradles to raise and lower scenery from the grid.

CYCLORAMA   Otherwise known as the sky-cloth, hung over the stage and lit to imply limitless space and distance; removeable, but often left in situ, doing no harm and being out of the way.

DADO   Area of wall between the chair-rail and skirting, separately decorated.

DENTIL   Close-set cubes resembling teeth, usually in Ionic or Corinthian Orders.

DORIC   First order of Greek architecture; see also Ionic, Corinthian.

DORMER   Window formed within a roof slope, deriving its name from sleeping quarters.

DROP-BEAM   A ceiling beam protruding below the general level of the major surface.

EGG AND DART   Classical strip ornament, resembling eggs separated by dart-like forms.

EMPIRE STYLE   A neo-classical style that developed in France during the Napoleonic years at the beginning of the 19th century.

ENTABLATURE   Upper part of a classical order comprising architrave, frieze and cornice.

FASCIA   Vertical face, part of the entablature of a classical order.

FLAT   Used in pairs to form two halves of a back-scene, constructed to be drawn off stage to left and right.

FREE CLASSICAL   A mixture of classical styles associated with the later 19th century.

FRIEZE   In a classical entablature, the plain central horizontal band.

GARLAND   Festoon or wreath ornament of leaves and flowers.

GLAZED BRICK   Enamel or ceramic coat applied to the face of bricks and fixed by a second kiln firing.

GRAVE TRAP   On the stage, beneath the centre line of the proscenium arch; the trap derives its name from its use in the grave scene of *Hamlet*.

GRID   An open timber floor sited high above the stage allowing hemps supporting flying scenery to pass through.

GROOVES   Upper and lower grooves that supported flats and wings, enabling them to be slid on and off stage. The most important surviving set were rescued from the Theatre Royal, Leicester.

GROTESQUE   Classical ornament related to the Arabesque, but including animals and figures.

GUILLOCHE   Classical strip ornament comprising interlaced circles.

GUTTAE   Small cylindrical pendant drops on the underside of mutules.

IONIC   Second order of Greek architecture; see also Doric, Corinthian.

LOUIS XIV   Architectural style associated with the French king Louis XIV (1643–1715).

LOUIS XV   Rococo style characteristic of the period of the French king Louis XV (1715–74).

MANSARD   A roof formed as two slopes, the lower slope being steep with a flatter upper part, often housing dormer windows.

MARGENT   Linked vertical flowers and husks, generally suspended from a bow or patera.

MODILLION   Projecting bracket carrying the upper members of a cornice.

MUTULE   Flat blocks on the underside of a cornice, decorated with guttae and set on the centreline of triglyphs.

O. P. SIDE   Generally stage right, i.e. that half of the stage to the actors' right. The acronym comes from 'opposite prompt', the prompt box traditionally being stage left.

PALMETTE   Stylized palm leaf or honeysuckle flower.

PATERA   Generally circular 'plates', often ornamented to represent a flower.

PEDIMENT   Triangular wall above a classical entablature, masking the roof slope.

PENDENTIVE   Triangular curving surface by which a circular dome is supported above a right-angled compartment.

PILASTER   Shallow rectangular projection representing a classical column.

PLINTH   Square block member at the base of a column; also used to describe the base of a building.

PORTICO   Colonnaded, roofed area forming entrance or vestibule, and supported by regularly spaced columns on at least one side.

PROMPT SIDE   Generally stage left, i.e. that half of the stage to the actors' left. The prompt box is traditionally situated on this side.

PULVINATED   From *pulvinus* = pillow or cushion (Latin): a convex frieze.

REEDING   Decorative moulding derived from the appearance of bunched parallel reeds.

REGENCY   Architectural period extending roughly from the later 1790s to the 1830s, when George, Prince of Wales (later King George IV) was Prince Regent.

RINCEAU   Classical continuous leafy scrolled foliage ornament.

RUSTICATION   Emphasized chamfered 'V' joints cut into stonework to suggest additional strength.

SCAGLIOLA   Imitation marble.

SLIDER   Sections of stage floor dropped and drawn off, to be replaced by a bridge or slote.

SLOTE   A backboard with fixed spacers and facing pieces to which groundrows etc. could be attached and winched through slots in the stage; generally found in pairs and between bridges.

SPANDREL   The approximate triangle formed by the head of an arch and its vertical plane.

STAGE RAKE   Generally assumed to be a slope of about 1 in 24, and believed to provide the audience with an improved view of the action. Of all the Edwardian and Victorian West End theatres, only Her Majesty's has a flat stage.

STUCCO   Smooth finished, fine lime plaster, often coloured to represent stonework, now invariably painted.

SUNBURST   Radiating beams around a central face, having an ecclesiastical flavour.

THEATRE FIRES   Common occurrences between the late 18th and late 19th centuries, during which time the average life of a theatre was about 18–20 years.

TUSCAN   Simplified Roman Doric order.

THUNDER RUN   Usually consisting of two or more long inclined timber troughs down which iron balls could be rolled to produce the effect of thunder.

TRIGLYPH   Three grooved blocks, representing stylized beam-ends, in a Doric frieze.

TROPHY   Arms and armour displayed as a sculpted celebration of victory.

TYMPANUM   Triangular face of a pediment within the sloping and horizontal moulded cornices.

VESTIBULE   Lobby or ante-room immediately behind the main entrance door to a building.

VICTORIAN   Architectural period coinciding with the reign of Queen Victoria (1837–1901).

WING   A canvas-covered flat based at the side of the stage, generally at right angles and worked in and out by means of grooves.

SELECT BIBLIOGRAPHY

Atwell, David, *Cathedrals of the Movies* (The Architectural Press, 1980)

Cherry, Bridget and Pevsner, Nikolaus, *Buildings of England, London, 2: South* (Penguin Books, 1984)

Cherry, Bridget and Pevsner, Nikolaus, *Buildings of England, London, 4: North* (Penguin Books, 1998)

Fletcher, Sir Banister, *A History of Architecture on the Comparative Method* (Batsford, 1954)

Fleetwood, Frances, *Conquest: The Story of a Theatre Family* (W. H. Allen, 1953)

Glasstone, Victor, *Victorian and Edwardian Theatres* (Thames & Hudson, 1975)

Howard, Diana, *London Theatres and Music Halls, 1850–1950* (The Library Association, 1970)

Leacroft, Richard, *The Development of the English Playhouse (*Methuen, 1973)

Leacroft, Richard and Helen, *Theatre and Playhouse (*Methuen, 1984)

Mander, Raymond and Mitchenson, Joe, *Theatres of London* (New English Library, 1975)

Pevsner, Nikolaus, revised by Cherry, Bridget *Buildings of England, London, 1: The Cities of London and Westminster* (Penguin Books, 1973)

Sachs, Edwin O., *Modern Opera Houses and Theatres* (3 vols) (London, 1896–98)

Sheppard, Francis H. W., ed., *The Survey of London*, vols 29, 34, 36 (London, Greater London Council)

Trevelyan, George Macaulay, *Illustrated English Social History* (Pelican Books, 1964)

Walker, Brian, ed., *Frank Matcham: Theatre Architect (*Blackstaff Press, 1980)

INDEX

ACKNOWLEDGEMENTS

The existence of this book is due entirely to the help, advice and goodwill of many people. My visits to the 53 West End theatres described here must have been, at best, an inconvenience to the owners, management and staff of buildings that are in almost constant daily use. In every case I was made welcome, and my questions were answered with clarity and endless patience. For all of this, and more, my heartfelt thanks.

To Richard Leacroft I owe an unpayable debt of gratitude. He more than anyone opened my eyes, as a student of his in the late 1950s, to the architecture of the theatre, and to its mechanical intricacies and foibles. He brought home to me the irreplaceable value of the many theatres that were being demolished by local councils and big business, without thought or conscience, during the 1950s and 1960s. I hope that this book will prove that I was listening!

To John Earl, former director of the Theatres Trust, I owe a special 'thank you'. Without his faith the opportunity to write this book would never have arisen. I must also thank Mike Stock at English Heritage, for his time, willingly given, in verifying and checking references.

Although they were not directly involved with this book, I would like to thank the Historians Group of the Historic Buildings Division within the former Greater London Council, who unreservedly shared an amazing breadth of knowledge and depth of research, not only on theatres but on many other diverse matters, between 1970 and 1986, when the group was slowly dematerialized after being absorbed into English Heritage.

To my wife, Sue, a tremendous 'thank you', not only for her patience and understanding but also in recognition of the fact that without her typing expertise, combined with the computer skills of my son and daughter-in-law, Simon and Karen, along with Inez Wilkins, the battle might have been lost.

Finally, I would like to pay special tribute to the memory of the many, often young, performers who lost their lives in theatre fires, not only in London, but throughout the British Isles.

MIKE KILBURN

I dedicate my work in this book to Isabel del Río for her crucial support and assistance in the production of the photography of *London's Theatres*.

I would also like to praise the invaluable help and assistance of the management and technical staff of all the theatres included in this book.

My thanks also to María Luisa Kara-Susán, Emilio Arzoz and James Morris.

ALBERTO ARZOZ